WHEN

CHURCHYARDS

YAWN

and Other Plays

by Jeanmarie Simpson

Upstage Left Press

First Edition · 2025

First Edition, 2025

ISBN: 979-8-9989008-0-8

Published by Upstage Left Press

Printed in the United States of America

For performance rights and inquiries, contact:

upstageleftpress@gmail.com

For Michael, Lynnie, Sean and Gary.

For Cassie, in heaven.

For the ones who stayed.

For the ones who couldn't.

And for Tate.

ACKNOWLEDGMENTS

These four plays did not come from me in the way my others have. They arrived—urgent, whole, and often uninvited—during a time when everything else was unraveling.

The Pandemic changed the way I write, and what I write. These plays felt channeled. *When Churchyards Yawn* emerged from a single moment: Zefirelli's Hamlet on television, the walls closing in, and the unmistakable sense that we were all trapped in Purgatory. The others—*Ghosts of the Gilded Stage, Lear (a solo adaptation)*, and *Even Unto Death*—came like wildfire.

To those who received these works in their rawest forms and helped me craft them into what they are now—thank you.

Michael Rawley, Lynne Griffin, Sean Sullivan, Gary Wright, and Tate—I don't know what these plays would be without your time, attention, care, and your honesty. And I'm grateful I'll never have to find out.

To Arizona Theatre Matters—my artistic home, my constant challenge, and my heartbeat.

To Dan. Thank you for holding steady while the storm wrote through me.

To those we've lost, especially Cassie. Your absence echoes in every silence between lines.

This book is a record of survival—not just mine, but something older, deeper, and shared.

If these words find you, may they move through you, too.

- *Jeanmarie Simpson, May 9, 2025*

TABLE OF CONTENTS

WHEN CHURCHYARDS YAWN

CHARACTERS

GATEKEEPER - Hard-boiled. Wears reading glasses on a chain. Carries clipboard and quill.

HAMLET SR. - Ancient. Exhausted.

POLONIUS - Ancient. Befuddled.

ROSENCRANTZ - Feels like a nitwit.

GUILDENSTERN - Blames Rosencrantz.

OPHELIA - Innocent and furious.

GERTRUDE - Spitting mad.

CLAUDIUS - Younger than HAMLET SR., closer to Hamlet's age. Nauseatingly contrite.

LAERTES - Charming. Codependent as hell.

HAMLET - Last to arrive.

SETTING

Purgatory. Sometime later.

NOTE FROM THE PLAYWRIGHT

If you don't know Shakespeare's *Hamlet*, please read it. At least the student guides or Wikipedia plot description or some such. Watch Zefirelli's *Hamlet*, if you can find it. Then read this play, otherwise you're not going to know what's going on, and you may feel grouchy. - JMS

SCENE 1

DUMB SHOW

Soundscape of serenity and dread—think Prokofiev's "Dance of the Knights" —morphing into something celestial and strange. The stage is cluttered with medieval detritus: wagons, skeletons, farming gear, torn books, chamber pots, lutes, crucifixes, and strange forgotten things. A chaos of humanity's leftovers.

Unbeknownst to the audience, the clutter will become a staircase—uneven, handmade—that leads to the blue double doors upstage. For now, it's just junk.

HAMLET SR. enters alone, in silhouette. He tries, repeatedly, to shim a wobbly table leg with small scraps of wood. It keeps failing. He gives up, tries again. A metaphor.

Slowly, the others begin to wander in. All except HAMLET. Lost. Frightened. Except OPHELIA, who floats. GATEKEEPER enters briskly, clipboard in hand, all business.

GATEKEEPER spots OPHELIA. Walks her to the blue portal—Heaven—via some strange pulley contraption. OPHELIA hesitates. She looks in... then floats gently back to stage level.

GATEKEEPER is appalled. OPHELIA rejoins the others. CLAUDIUS sees HAMLET SR. and crosses to him. He kneels, head bowed. HAMLET SR. draws a sword, raises it over CLAUDIUS's head. Pauses. Lowers it. Helps him up. They embrace. GERTRUDE watches, emotionally eviscerated.

GATEKEEPER crosses downstage center. She pulls off her reading glasses. Looks directly at us.

GATEKEEPER
'Tis now the very witching time of night when churchyards yawn, and Hell itself breathes out contagion to this world.

GERTRUDE
Now could I drink hot blood, and do such bitter business as the day would quake to look on.

OPHELIA
Thou know'st 'tis common: All that lives must die, passing through nature to eternity.

HAMLET
(entering, bewildered) So do we charge Your Royal Highness
Upon the view and knowing of these contents—

LAERTES
I do wish that your good beauties
Be the happy cause of Hamlet's wildness.

HAMLET
…without debatement further more or less,
To put those bearers, Guildenstern and Rosencrantz, to sudden death—

HAMLET SR.
A violet in the youth of primy nature.

POLONIUS
'Tis an unweeded garden that grows to seed.

HAMLET SR.
Things rank and gross in nature possess it merely.

HAMLET
As peace should still her wheaten garland wear,
And stand a comma 'tween our amities.

CLAUDIUS
There is no ancient gentleman but gardeners, ditchers, and grave-makers.

LAERTES
They hold up Adam's profession.

HAMLET
No shriving-time allowed.

> *A beat of silence.*

GUILDENSTERN
Oh, feculence.

ROSENCRANTZ
Bugger.

> *GATEKEEPER yanks a desk from the pile, drags it stage left, sits. This is now processing. Like it's the DMV of the damned.*

GATEKEEPER
Okay, everybody—line up!

> *They line up in order: OPHELIA, GUILDENSTERN, ROSENCRANTZ, POLONIUS, LAERTES, HAMLET SR., CLAUDIUS, GERTRUDE. HAMLET lingers behind, stunned.*

GATEKEEPER *(not looking up)*
Name?

OPHELIA
I was called Ophelia.

GATEKEEPER
And what keeps you in *purgatorius ignis*, lady?
You're assigned to Heaven.

OPHELIA
All my loved ones are here.

GATEKEEPER
All?

OPHELIA
My father and brother...

GATEKEEPER
And?

OPHELIA
(pause) The prince.

GATEKEEPER
There are no princes here, lady.

OPHELIA
But—

GATEKEEPER
What name, lady?

OPHELIA
He was my lord.

GATEKEEPER
No lords in Purgatory.

GERTRUDE
(snaps) WE CALLED HIM HAMLET.

GATEKEEPER
Ah. Yes. *Hamlet.*
(scribbles, looks up at OPHELIA) What shall I do with you?
(pause, decision made) Take a seat.

>   *GUILDENSTERN drags a chair forward.*
>   *OPHELIA sits beside the desk.*

GATEKEEPER
Name?

GUILDENSTERN
They called me Guildenstern.

GATEKEEPER
(looks up at him) Your mother named you *Guildenstern?*

GUILDENSTERN
No, she—
(scratches his head) I don't remember what my mother named me.
But I know I was called Guildenstern.

GATEKEEPER
(scribbles) Guildenstern.
(consults a list) Hmmm… it appears you're on the cusp
'twixt here— *(points toward red portal)*
—and there.

GUILDENSTERN
(terrified) There? But that's—
I mean, that's got to be—
Are you sure?

GATEKEEPER
Start a line there. *(gestures up center)*

GUILDENSTERN
(deep breath, mutters) Brilliant.

GATEKEEPER
NEXT.

> *ROSENCRANTZ steps up, a little too chipper, trying to hide his fear.*

ROSENCRANTZ
They called me Rosencrantz, that did speak of me.
I'm pretty sure my Christian name was Frederik,
but no one called me that.

GATEKEEPER
(scribbles) Very good. *(gestures toward GUILDENSTERN)*

ROSENCRANTZ
Can you double-check?

GATEKEEPER
NEXT.

> *POLONIUS steps up, nervously smoothing his robes.*

POLONIUS
Hello.

GATEKEEPER
And you are?

POLONIUS
Lord Chamberlain to the court of good King Hamlet of Denmark,
subsequently to his brother, King Claudius.

Lord Chamberlain— *(sees she's not impressed)*
I was called Polonius.

GATEKEEPER
(checks list, nods toward upstage line) Join the crowd.

POLONIUS
Oh no—there must be some mistake, surely?

GATEKEEPER *(double-checks)*
Nope.
All your sins are on your head as we speak.
Go.

> POLONIUS *shuffles off, confused. OPHELIA*
> *watches, stricken.*

LAERTES
(approaches suavely) Hello.

GATEKEEPER
Name?

LAERTES
Guess.

GATEKEEPER
(deadpan) Are you insane?

LAERTES
(smiling) Smitten, is what I am.

GATEKEEPER
Not entirely irritated yet.
What is your name?

LAERTES
Call me Orpheus—

GATEKEEPER
Your name in life, man.

POLONIUS
(From upstage) Laertes!

GATEKEEPER
(to POLONIUS) Thank you.
(to LAERTES) Your mother and he named you Laertes.
(checks her list) Join your father.

LAERTES
Can't I stay here with you?
And my sister?

GATEKEEPER
(to OPHELIA) Was he always such a pest?

OPHELIA
I'm not sure.

GATEKEEPER
(to LAERTES) Get moving.

LAERTES
Oh, lady—

GATEKEEPER
NEXT.

> *LAERTES winks at her and saunters away.*
> *HAMLET SR. steps up, trying not to show nerves.*

HAMLET SR.
I was the king.

GATEKEEPER
Was being operative.

We've been over and over this.
There are no kings here.
You are not special.
Now go join the others—or go to Hell.

HAMLET SR.
But—

GATEKEEPER
You've got almost no time
to either join the others
or be forever damned.
Your choice.
NEXT!

> HAMLET SR. *sighs deeply, shuffles toward the others.*
> CLAUDIUS *steps forward.*

CLAUDIUS
I'm—

GATEKEEPER
(cuts him off, disgusted) I know who you are.
What are you doing here?

(points to red portal) Go!

> GERTRUDE *blocks his path.*

GERTRUDE
Please!
May I petition on his behalf?

GATEKEEPER
No—

GERTRUDE
Please, please, *please.*

GATEKEEPER
Why?

GERTRUDE
I don't know.
I can't explain it.
I just can't bear to part with him.

GATEKEEPER
Then go with him.

OPHELIA
Oh no—PLEASE!

GATEKEEPER
What is your concern?

OPHELIA
The Queen—

GATEKEEPER
No queens in Purgatory.

OPHELIA
She is the mother of—

> *A bell rings at the desk. GATEKEEPER picks up a funky earpiece and a cone, which she speaks into.*

GATEKEEPER
Hello? *(listens)*
As you will, Your Grace. *(hangs up)*

(to CLAUDIUS, begrudgingly) Very well. Stand with the others.
But watch it, pal.
You're on the thinnest ice there ever was.
(to GERTRUDE) Gerutha, is it?

GERTRUDE
Yuck.
Gertrude, please.

GATEKEEPER
(scribbles) Gertrude.
(points to line) NE—

HAMLET
Hamlet.

>   *A long pause. GATEKEEPER slowly puts on her*
>   *glasses, double-checks the list.*

GATEKEEPER
Oh dear, dear, dear, dear, dear.
You are all over the map.
What a mess.
(to OPHELIA) What do you think?

OPHELIA
Methinks he must explain himself.
(suddenly furious) He behaved *dreadfully.*

GATEKEEPER
And yet, you stay for him.

OPHELIA
Ugh!
I was a little fool in life,
and I'm an idiot now!

GATEKEEPER
No, lady. You're not an idiot.
You have a good and gentle heart.
Of all these souls, it's you who are called by the angels.

OPHELIA
If the angels knew how foul my mood has become
just looking at him, they'd—
Well. What now?

GATEKEEPER
Now, we take on the gates.

ALL
(shudder in fear) No!
Oh no—
Not the gates!
Saints preserve us!
Oh, God, save us!

HAMLET *(squeaks)*
The gates?!

GATEKEEPER
The gates.
Or portals, if you will.

HAMLET
(sees CLAUDIUS) ACK!
(points) What's *he* doing here?!

LAERTES
I don't get it either.
But look at *you*—you're here.
And you killed most of these people.

HAMLET
I didn't mean to—

LAERTES
Oh yeah, you did.
You meant to kill Claudius when you killed my father,
killed Ophelia by being an ass and driving her mad,
killed Rosencrantz and Guildenstern by tricking the English,
killed your mother by not drinking from the cup meant for you,
straight-up stabbed Claudius in the gut,
and then *poisoned* him,
and you *sliced me from stem to stern.*

HAMLET
You stabbed *me* with a poisoned blade!

LAERTES
Well, yes.
But we made up before we died.

HAMLET
And Claudius murdered my father!
(crosses to HAMLET SR.) Hey! What are you doing here?!
You told me you were confined to fast in fires
'til the foul crimes done in your days of nature
were burnt and purged away!

HAMLET SR.
I was speaking *metaphorically.*

> HAMLET *lunges toward CLAUDIUS.*
> LAERTES *pulls him aside.*

LAERTES
Steady, old man.

HAMLET
(gesturing toward CLAUDIUS) Look at him!
What the hell is *he* doing here?!
(pause, then quieter) I suppose I should say hello to my mother.

LAERTES
You can try.

HAMLET
(crosses to GERTRUDE) Hello, my mother.

GERTRUDE
(dry) Oh, look who's here.

HAMLET
(to LAERTES) I'm lost.
(suddenly realizing) And *so thirsty!*

LAERTES
So am I.

ALL THE REST
Me too!

HAMLET SR.
You get used to it.

They all look at him desperately.

HAMLET
How?!

HAMLET SR.
I don't know.
Soon you let go of the panic
and give in to unadulterated despair.

ROSENCRANTZ
(rises, crosses right) I can't stand this!

HAMLET
(crosses after him) My excellent good friend!
How do you, Guildenstern?

ALL EXCEPT HAMLET
Rosencrantz!

HAMLET
(whoops) Free me so far in your most generous thoughts
that I have shot mine arrow o'er the house
and hurt my brother—
gentle Rosencrantz.

> *ROSENCRANTZ stares at him. Beat. Then huffs
> over to GUILDENSTERN.*

HAMLET SR.
(crosses to HAMLET, puts an arm around him) Sit down, my boy.
Take a load off.

HAMLET
Huh?

HAMLET SR.
Relax.
Take a seat.

> *Guides HAMLET to sit on the pile of clutter.*

HAMLET
My liege—

HAMLET SR.
Take me for all in all,
I am a ghost.

HAMLET
A ghost?

HAMLET SR.
Ghost, spirit, specter, spook, phantom, apparition...
The point is—there are no kings here.
No princes.

GATEKEEPER
It's a level field—

HAMLET SR.
No head—

GATEKEEPER
No foot—

HAMLET SR.
A round field.

GATEKEEPER
(imperiously) Annular.

HAMLET SR.
Not one of us received last rites.
And we've all got issues with each other.

OPHELIA
And ourselves.

HAMLET SR.
Therefore—we can't get out of here
until we've all made it through the seven gates.

GATEKEEPER
And you must all make peace with each other
and yourselves before you can leave.
It's a package deal.

OPHELIA
What does that mean?

GATEKEEPER
We share a connection.
Living, breathing, celestial biology unites us all.
We are not puppets of life—we *are* life.
Souls that have existed for eons,
interconnected worlds pretending to be separate universes.
We are to the world as waves to the ocean —
small, human-shaped waves
moving through the cosmic sea.
It is up to us to find our way home.
And without each other, we are lost.
Now that you, Ophelia, have chosen to stay,
you are stuck.
Either you *all* make it to Heaven—
or you are *all* damned to Hell.
Got it?
OPHELIA
(shocked) But—

GATEKEEPER
No buts.
That's the way it goes.
You're not separate.
You're all one.

HAMLET
So, you are saying—

GATEKEEPER
We move in soul pods.

HAMLET
Huh?!

LAERTES
"Soul pods"??
GATEKEEPER
Yes.
We're sent to Earth in clusters,
and in clusters we must move into the hereafter.
Our lives are woven into each the other's.
Do you see?

GERTRUDE
If we're all one, how can *some* be damned?

GATEKEEPER
It's a mystery.

GERTRUDE
Okay, but—

GATEKEEPER
Infinity is circular.
The outer reaches are Heaven.
The center is Hell.

GERTRUDE
Okay, but—

GATEKEEPER
The outside is exquisite—pure Grace.
The center is a boiling inferno
where joy cannot survive.

GERTRUDE
Okay, but—

GATEKEEPER
Mysteries cannot be explained.
They can only be experienced.
The best I can do
is tell you that the outside relies on the center for warmth,
as a home does a hearth fire —
but no one wants to *sleep in the flames.*

> GERTRUDE *opens her mouth, starts to speak again,*
> *then stops.*
> *All fall into introspection. Silence. Then HAMLET*
> *steps forward.*

HAMLET
(to the audience, unheard by the others) We are all one?
Where is *that* in the Catechism?
Can it be that Ophelia's salvation depends on mine?
That *mine* depends on my *uncle's? incredulous—then horrified*
Scripture tells us we're to love our brothers as ourselves.
But our *uncle?*
Our slimy, piece of rat-excrement uncle?!
He that mercilessly killed our father?!
He that—
(realizes) Oh God.
My *mother's* salvation depends on *his.*
My *father's* too—
my father whom he murdered most torturously...
This is ludicrous.
The best of these people
are no more likely to see Heaven
than the most evil among us?
(looks back at the group) Huh.
Okay then.

(deep breath) This has to be done.

Let it be.

What's the alternative?

Stay here forever?

Go to Hell?

God forbid.

And to think I once believed in destiny.

I felt helpless then.

I feel more helpless now.

(looks at CLAUDIUS) Who's to say what *he'll* do?

He can't be trusted.

ARGH! This is agony!

(pause) No point whining about it.

Come on, courage —

take me over this cliff

and give me faith that when I land,

I won't be smashed to bits

but lifted up...

And with me —

my mother,

my father,

my love,

her father,

her brother,

and my friends.

God help me.

(returns to the others) Why was I the last one to the party?

(to LAERTES) We died at the same time, didn't we?

LAERTES

You were on the brink of death for a while.

HAMLET

I don't remember any of that.

HAMLET SR.
You were out cold
for some time
before you fully died.
Count your lucky stars, my boy.
I don't want to rehash the past,
but this one—*(gestures toward CLAUDIUS)*
—in the porches of mine ears
did pour the leperous distilment,
and I felt every bit of it
until there wasn't enough left of my insides
to spread on a biscuit.

CLAUDIUS
I do apologize again, Your Grace.

HAMLET SR.
I'm just trying to get the kid to look on the bright side.

GERTRUDE
Hamlet, you are the lucky one.
I died a gruesome death, as you witnessed—

POLONIUS
—and you stabbed me through the tapestry—

OPHELIA
—which took me to my wits' end
and I more or less lost my mind and—

LAERTES
—fell in the creek,
singing old church songs...

GERTRUDE
—and, sadly, fell asleep and drowned...

LAERTES
—which led me to avenge
my father and sister's untimely deaths...

ROSENCRANTZ
Speaking of untimely—

GUILDENSTERN
We honestly had no idea—

ROSENCRANTZ
We had just arrived—

GUILDENSTERN
Hadn't even unpacked—

ROSENCRANTZ
He was the king—

GUILDENSTERN
We were his *subjects*—

ROSENCRANTZ
—and he gave us the letter—

GUILDENSTERN
—with the royal *seal*—

ROSENCRANTZ
—to take with us to England.

GUILDENSTERN
We had no way of knowing—

ROSENCRANTZ
It was unreasonable of you to expect us to—

GUILDENSTERN
He was the *KING,* after all.

ROSENCRANTZ
We were beheaded—

GUILDENSTERN
Unshriven—

ROSENCRANTZ
Unannealed—

GUILDENSTERN
Seems a *bit* harsh—

HAMLET
(throws up his hands, stands, crosses down right) STOP!

OPHELIA
(crosses to HAMLET, grabs and twists his ear) You are NOT THE BOSS!

HAMLET
(rubbing his ear, running away) OW!
(runs to GERTRUDE) Mother—

GERTRUDE
Oh, you *are* funny.

HAMLET SR.
(grabs HAMLET by his other ear) Getting back to the point—

GATEKEEPER
You have all been in Limbo,
save your father —
who's been here a long, *long* time.

We've had a backlog.
No one remembers Limbo —
but it's actually quite a delightful experience.
Purgatory's the worst.

HAMLET
Worse than Hell?

GATEKEEPER
In Hell, you *know* where you are.
You *know* you'll never leave.
Here —
you *might* end up in the inferno,
or you *might* make it to the end of the rainbow.
It's very stressful.

POLONIUS
Oh, my nerves.

HAMLET SR.
Rainbows that break the law end up going to *prism*.

GERTRUDE
(SO over him) Your father has been here the longest.
And he really needs to go.
So you must listen to him
and do what he says.

HAMLET SR.
Not because I'm your father—
but because—

GERTRUDE
He's an insufferable bore
and if he doesn't—

HAMLET SR.
Gertrude—

GERTRUDE
(holds up her hand, turns away) Stop.
You were off doing king things
 and I was a teenage queen
 left alone with honey wine and embroidery hoops.

CLAUDIUS
You were innocent, Gertrude.
I was the lecherous villain.

GERTRUDE
I didn't protest enough.
But you might have stopped me
from drinking that bloody poisoned cup!

CLAUDIUS
I—

HAMLET SR.
Bottom line, son —
before I can leave,
you need to address your daddy issues.

GERTRUDE
And he *really* needs to leave.

HAMLET SR.
(to GERTRUDE, with attitude) Believe me, honey—

HAMLET
(cuts him off) What do we need to do?

GATEKEEPER
(pulls a chart from the pile, hangs it in sight. She finds a pointer.) There are seven

levels.

Terraces.

Gates, if you will.

You must travel through each

  to reach the outer portal on the other side.

Which leads to the portals

  over there, and up there—

The portals light up, open, play music. Ominous. Beautiful.

HAMLET
I'm the only one who has to do this?

OPHELIA
Try to keep up.

GERTRUDE
Really, darling.

GATEKEEPER
Pay attention.

HAMLET
(gulps) Where are these gates, terraces, or levels,
  if you will?

GATEKEEPER
You must build them.

To get to any of them,

you must turn this miscellany into a ladder of sorts.

Each level gets you closer to the next.

Observe.

(She flips a page on the chart. It's grotesque and divine.)

To face *Gluttony,*

  you must first confront *Lust.*

To contend with *Sloth,*

  you must first grapple with *Avarice.*

Before facing *Envy,*
 you must embrace *Wrath.*
And finally —
you must come to terms with *Pride.*

HAMLET
Those are the Seven Deadly Sins.

OPHELIA
And you excelled at them all.

HAMLET
I thought Pride was first.

OPHELIA
Says who?

HAMLET
I learned it in school.

OPHELIA
From whom?

HAMLET
Um… teachers…

OPHELIA
Listen up, *clotpole—*

> *HAMLET cowers toward GERTRUDE.*

GERTRUDE
Your teachers were mortal, son.
Whoever got the message
heard it upside down, apparently.

POLONIUS
No point arguing.
There's no changing it.
We start with *Lust*.

A loud gavel CRACK from
GATEKEEPER.
The junkpile lets out a low mechanical
groan—a heavy plank shifts visibly on its own.
A red light begins to swell underfoot.
Heat. Pressure. Something in the air tightens.

Everyone reacts differently: a stagger, a breath
held, a wary look at each other.

The soundscape hums with dissonance—not
music, but almost.
LUST has begun to rise.

GATEKEEPER steps forward.

SCENE 2

> *Red light rises. It's hot. Thick. The air itself seems to sweat. The characters begin to pull pieces from the pile, creating the first level of the structure.*

GATEKEEPER
(To Gertrude) Take it away, lady. LUST!
(Bangs a gavel.)

GERTRUDE
(Starts sorting through the pile, finding things to create a level up. Takes a deep breath, addresses Hamlet.) You said to me, "At your age, the heyday in the blood is tame, it's humble and waits upon the judgment."

HAMLET
(Crosses to Gertrude) Yes.

> *Awkward pause.*

HAMLET SR.
He was always a little high strung.

GERTRUDE
(To Hamlet) You called me an old bag and shamed me in my own room, on my own bed.
Self-entitled little brat!

CLAUDIUS
You were pretty rough on your mother, son. The whole "rank sweat, enseamèd bed, stewed in corruption, making love over the nasty sty" business.

GERTRUDE
RIGHT??

POLONIUS
This is very embarrassing.

ROSENCRANTZ
Um… can we—

GUILDENSTERN
Where're we gonna go?

OPHELIA
Hush, you two!

LAERTES
(To Ophelia) This is intense.

OPHELIA
Be quiet!

GERTRUDE
Have you any idea how old I was???

HAMLET
Sixty?

GERTRUDE
(Smacks him on the chest) I was THIRTY-FIVE, you spoiled rotten little LIZARD! *(Continues to smack him.)*

HAMLET
(Puts up his arms to block the blows) I didn't know!
CLAUDIUS
(Tries to comfort Gertrude) He led a sheltered life.

GERTRUDE

Stay out of this!

(To Hamlet) LISTEN to me, you! You were my only child, and you were
the prince and you had everything handed to you on a golden salver
from the time you were 18 seconds old! Your father barely touched me
after you were born.

HAMLET

But, you hung on him—

GERTRUDE

(Starts handing things to Claudius) Of course, I did! Was I to allow the
masses to see me for the *de facto* cuckqueen I was??

All he cared about was having an heir and being KING!

Every morning he was combed, dressed, and outfitted. His chaplain
brought him his breviary and helped him say his hours.

Then he went to mass, after which he was met by a crowd of
commoners—rich, poor, ladies, maidens, widows, and every other piece
of smelly riffraff that had problems.

He kindly granted them whatever they asked because GOD FORBID
anyone didn't LIKE him.

He spent all his time either where he was seen and kibitzed with the
general public, or where he was seen with his pretty relatives and
courtiers, or on his own with the servants ALWAYS in earshot—except
when he took a nap in the orchard and snored like a syphilitic bear.

After dinner, he insisted on appearing among both the commoners
AND his court when he would meet with various lofty officials.

Finally, he would sup with his Royal Council.

By that time, I was DONE with an extra-tall vessel of honey wine and
the needlework of the day and PASSED OUT IN MY CHAMBER!

POLONIUS

(To Hamlet) That's where you stabbed me.

GERTRUDE

(Daggers) Wait your turn, old man.

HAMLET
(*Beginning to sort through the stuff*) Mother, I—

GERTRUDE
Your uncle gave me attention.
He complimented my hair and features and brought me flowers after
you were born. For a long time. FOR TWENTY YEARS!
He TALKED to me, and what's more, he LISTENED to me.
My GOD, I was a TEENAGER,
and I wouldn't have known a choice if it PUNCHED ME IN THE
EYE.
My marriage to your father was arranged before I was even BORN.
When your father died, and I married your uncle—granted, three and a
half weeks isn't much of a mourning period—but, dammit, I was FREE.
For the first time in my entire life, I got to make a CHOICE of my own,
and I chose HIM.

HAMLET
He killed your husband.
GERTRUDE
I didn't know that! Did you know it?
(*Turns to the others*) Did you know it?

Everyone shakes their heads, mumbles, shrugs, etc.

HAMLET
Nobody knew it THEN—
GERTRUDE
Oh, but you felt entitled to shame me and carry on about what a saint
your father was.
He wasn't a saint!
He may have been a lovely father to you, but he was a HORRIBLE
husband to me.

HAMLET
But once I'd told you—

GERTRUDE
You were talking to the wallpaper! I thought you were a fruitbat!

HAMLET
My father's ghost was in the room.

GERTRUDE
Well, he didn't do me the courtesy of materializing so that I could see
him, did he?

HAMLET
Mother, I'm sorry.

GERTRUDE
(Challenging him) For what are you sorry?

HAMLET
(Deep breath) I am sorry, Mother, that I didn't know—

GUILDENSTERN
Uh-oh.

GERTRUDE
That's a dodge.
HAMLET
(Sighs) What would you have me say?

GERTRUDE
Look into YOUR SOUL, and there you'll see such black and grainED
spots as will not leave their tinct.
You didn't care!
You wrote me off as a strumpet because I decided to have some

41

pleasure and some joy in my life.
Dear GOD, son —
EVERYTHING was not always about YOU!

The next four lines are said all at once.

OPHELIA
AMEN!

ROSENCRANTZ & GUILDENSTERN
Halleluia! HALLELUIA!

POLONIUS
BraVA!

LAERTES
(Clapping) Right on!

HAMLET
Okay, now, wait just a minute.
You were my mother. My nurses never told me any of this.
They insisted that the sun rose and set on me and that I was entitled to the moon.
My teachers never said a word about caring whether my mother was satisfied.
Perhaps as my MOTHER you might have put your oar into my upbringing.
When did I ever see you?
After lunch and at bedtime. For a couple of minutes.
At fairs and festivals when you deigned to put me on your lap—for SHOW, it always seemed to me.
Yorick was more of a mother to me than you.
He gave me piggyback rides every day!
He took the time with a little boy to teach him rhymes and riddles and songs.

He let me kiss him and hug him as much as I wanted.
He never sent me away.
But you—

CLAUDIUS
He makes some very good points.

GERTRUDE & HAMLET
Shut up!

CLAUDIUS
(Walks to the back of the crowd) Sorry.

CLAUDIUS
Well—doesn't he?

OPHELIA
He's so full of himself.
Either bragging or blaming everyone else for his problems.

LAERTES
But, Sister, he WAS raised to be a king, not a cobbler.

OPHELIA
 STOP making excuses for him!
HAMLET
How am I the bad guy here?

EVERYONE EXCEPT HAMLET
You KILLED US!

GERTRUDE
I want to get out of here.
It's your turn, kid. *(She steps up onto the platform she and Hamlet have made, extends her hand to him, helps him up.)*

HAMLET
My turn?

CLAUDIUS
Pull us through the flames of your lust issues with us.

HAMLET
One at a time?

ROSENCRANTZ
Whatever!

GUILDENSTERN
This is taking forEVER!

GATEKEEPER
HA!
What you don't know about forever—

HAMLET
Okay.
(To Rosencrantz and Guildenstern) I'll start with you.

You lusted after—what? Approval from the king?

> *Rosencrantz and Guildenstern start sorting through the stuff.*

ROSENCRANTZ
Disapproval wasn't exactly an option.

GUILDENSTERN
What would you have done in our place?

HAMLET
(Taking stuff from R&G as they hand it up) I would have been a loyal friend!
I would have TALKED to you, not snuck around conspiring—

GUILDENSTERN
ConSPIRING?!

ROSENCRANTZ
Your mother and the king asked us to find out what was up with you!

GUILDENSTERN
You had lost all your mirth.
What were we to DO?!

HAMLET
You might have mentioned that my mother and the king had sent for
you.

GUILDENSTERN
I was afraid—

ROSENCRANTZ
Me, too.
GATEKEEPER
Sit down, guys.

Rosencrantz and Guildenstern sit.

HAMLET
Laertes—Lust. Um…

LAERTES
 Nope.

(Crosses to R&G.) Deal me in, guys.
(He sits between them, looks over at Gatekeeper, points.) Who do you think she is?

ROSENCRANTZ
She does seem familiar.

LAERTES
Do you think there's romance in Heaven?

GUILDENSTERN
 I bet there is—

GERTRUDE
Are we done? Can I—

HAMLET
(Grossed out, but knows he has to get through it) No. I have… issues…

GERTRUDE
 Okay, what? *(She climbs off the platform and hands a bunch more stuff up to Hamlet.)*
HAMLET
It was gross seeing you slobbering all over my uncle so soon after my father died.

GERTRUDE
Yes, so you said.
(Pause) I apologize for not being more discreet.
Can I go now?

HAMLET
Is that really all there is to it?

GATEKEEPER
(To Gertrude) Feel better?

GERTRUDE
I'm exhausted!

GATEKEEPER
 Not finished.

HAMLET
I wanted you to be pure and chaste…
Mother, I'm sorry…
I didn't want you to be human.
I was a bad son—

GERTRUDE
Not always, Hamlet.
We had some good times.

HAMLET
There was that summer we put in the garden.
GERTRUDE
(Smiling, crossing to him) The garden. Yes.
(Kisses him on the cheek, puts her hand on his face.)

HAMLET
Remember how dirty we got, how the sweat dripped off my nose, and
when I wiped it with the back of my hand—

GERTRUDE
You looked like a mud puppy!
(Laughs) The earth beneath our fingernails.
I hated losing it in the bath.

Ophelia helps Gertrude back up onto the platform as Hamlet squares off with Polonius, who hands stuff up to him.

POLONIUS
I didn't like the way you looked at my daughter.

HAMLET
I didn't appreciate that you thought I only saw her through a lusty haze.

POLONIUS
I was young once.

HAMLET
You were not a prince.

POLONIUS
No—

HAMLET
I had all the girls in the kingdom to choose from, and it was Ophelia that
I—

POLONIUS
She was the most beautiful.

HAMLET
Think you so little of your daughter that she could only be loved for her face and eyes and bosom?

POLONIUS
I didn't believe, once you had your way with her, that you would be honorable.

HAMLET
I was the prince!
You were my father's advisor.
She wasn't some kitchen wench that I could anonymously ravish.

POLONIUS
I see. Well.
I may have underestimated you.

HAMLET
I'm sorry I stabbed you. I didn't mean it.

POLONIUS
Water under the bridge, dear boy.
(Shakes Hamlet's hand) Water under the bridge.

HAMLET
(To Ophelia) I am—

> *Ophelia throws things at him, which he hands to*
> *Gertrude, who organizes them unobtrusively.*

OPHELIA
Oh, let's not talk about what you are.
We know what you are.
We have established that you treated me like your own little rag doll sex toy, killed my father, stuffed him in an alcove, and sailed off to England. ASS!

HAMLET
(Squeaks) Sex toy?

OPHELIA
Let's review the unseemly things you said to me, shall we?
"...Never doubt I love. 'O dear Ophelia... I have not art to reckon my groans: but that I love you best, O most best, believe it."

Then you said you loved me ONCE, then in the next breath said you loved me not.

THEN, you said to get me to a nunnery!

Then, you put your head in my lap and made reference to CUNTry matters, "between a maid's legs," and you said you could interpret between me and my love, if you could see the puppets dallying."

What the hell did that mean?

HAMLET
I was confused.

OPHELIA
YOU were confused?! I—

HAMLET
I did not belong to you!

OPHELIA
I was young and my heart was cracked wide open.
I was easy prey for one who owned the world.
You had no right!

HAMLET
But all's fair in love—

OPHELIA
DON'T get cute with me.
I worshipped you!

HAMLET
And I you, lady.

OPHELIA
You had a helluva way of showing it.
You treated me like dirt!

HAMLET
I thought you trifled with me.
Your father and my uncle eavesdropped on us—you returned all the
pretty things I gave you.

OPHELIA
My father compelled me to!
I had no control over ANY of that!
Where was your chivalry?!
You blamed me for YOUR lust!
You blamed ME—

HAMLET
I was angry with you for the way you stirred my loins.
OPHELIA
(Throws something at his face) I never touched your loins!

HAMLET
But you—

OPHELIA
You should have taken it up with Nature.
I didn't do a damned thing but what was expected of me, and you drove
me insane and made me kill myself.

HAMLET
I thought you fell asleep in the water and drowned.

OPHELIA
I wouldn't have been in the water if you hadn't—

HAMLET
But, wait—if you had killed yourself, you couldn't be here, could you?
You'd be burning—

OPHELIA
I fell asleep and drowned.
That I was driven mad by your conduct puts my death squarely on your head.
(Pulls out a poppet, looks it in the face) Be that as it may—what are your lust issues with me?

HAMLET
Only that you drove me mad with wanting you.

OPHELIA
What could I have done differently?
HAMLET
(Pause) Ophelia—
(He raises his hand, hesitating.)

OPHELIA
(She flinches, then slaps his hand away.) Back off!
                    OPHELIA reaches up to Gertrude who pulls her up.

HAMLET
(Turns and watches Ophelia go, turns back and is nose to nose with Claudius) O villain, villain…

CLAUDIUS
Yes, Hamlet. In life, I was a villain.
Do your worst.

HAMLET
(Turns, looks at the pile) I don't know where to start.

CLAUDIUS
(Pulls out a large wooden wheelbarrow with a flat tire, starts putting things in it) I killed your parents…
Murdered your father to win your mother, and the crown.

HAMLET
(Puts something in the wheelbarrow) You lusted after my mother.

CLAUDIUS
Oh, yes. For more than 20 years.

HAMLET
(Continues putting things into the cart) You are a pig!

OPHELIA
Pig?

CLAUDIUS
I was a horrible man, you killed me, and I deserved it.

HAMLET
(To Gatekeeper) Why isn't he burning in Hell?

Ophelia glares at him.

GATEKEEPER
Your mother made an appeal, which was granted.
Don't ask me, I don't make the rules.

GERTRUDE
Grace, Hamlet.
Apparently, Grace is infinitely merciful.

HAMLET
That is just not FAIR!

OPHELIA
Worry about yourself!

CLAUDIUS
Here stand I before you, Hamlet.
Shall we get on with it?

HAMLET
You killed your brother and married his wife. That's incest, where I come from.

CLAUDIUS
And yet—

HAMLET
Well—what do you have to say for yourself?

CLAUDIUS
I was scum, a miscreant, a cad!
What CAN I say?
I was the lowest of the low, the most evil of them all, I deserve eternal damnation, yet HERE I AM.

HAMLET
(Pause) Are you sorry?

CLAUDIUS
Oh, yes.

HAMLET
(Turns to Gertrude) It's not enough!

GERTRUDE
I understand, but your father obviously got over it, and so must you, if we're to get out of here.

HAMLET
I'm not sure I can do that.

GATEKEEPER
Well, skip him for now.

HAMLET
(To Claudius) I'll get back to you.

> *Claudius crosses to a pile of books, organizes them.*
> *Sinister music rises.*

OPHELIA
(To HAMLET SR.) How did you raise such a son? A son who treated
his mother and lady love as if they were kitchen sluts?
HAMLET SR.
(Taken aback) I BEG your pardon?

OPHELIA
Oh, no question—in public he knew how to put on a show.
But where was your influence?
My father was forever giving my brother counsel—welcome or no, and
to me, too, which was weird because I was a girl and he was lost with
me.
But YOU!
How could you raise such a gross-mannered, ill-tempered son?!

LAERTES
He was Prince of Denmark…

OPHELIA
(Spins around and locks eyes with Laertes) And YOU!
I adored you.
I ran after you like a spaniel puppy, and you treated me like one.
Once I grew a bosom, all you did was tell me Hamlet couldn't marry me
and I shouldn't lose my virginity to him.
I mean—EW!

LAERTES
When you put it like that—

OPHELIA
I did the effect of your lessons keep as watchmen to my heart, and what good did it do me?!
LAERTES
 Oh, kind sister, sweet Ophelia! *(Tries to put his arms around her, but she thrusts at him a fireplace hand-bellows, which he hands to Polonius.)* Of all who failed you in life, I was surely the worst.
 You were perfection.

OPHELIA
I was NOT perfection. I was a girl!
You did me no service setting me up high where I had no bone, no blood, no heart, no flesh—

LAERTES
You were my dainty baby sister and none was amply gallant for you, especially not Hamlet.
I mean—I went to school with him.
I knew what a blackguard he was.

GERTRUDE & HAMLET
HEY!

GERTRUDE
The prince wasn't pure enough to marry your sister?!

LAERTES
I thought he was raising hell, making hay —
I figured you'd marry him off to the Princess of Leinster or Normandy or somewhere.

GERTRUDE
Never!
He was to marry for love.
LAERTES
Well, how was I supposed to know that?
OPHELIA
Hello!!!
LAERTES
(Ashamed) Sweet sister.
(Pause) I wasn't man enough to be a worthy brother for you.

OPHELIA
You were the only one I had!

LAERTES
I'm sorry.
(Pause) I'm so sorry.

HAMLET
How weary, stale, flat, and unprofitable seem to me—

OPHELIA
(Lunges at Hamlet, grabs him by the scruff of the neck) Mark me, you simpering
coward!
If I end up damned for all time, I will make it my personal mission to
see that you spend forever and ever smack dab in the middle of the
ninth circle where the Devil himself painstakingly devours your entrails
for a thousand eternities! *(She releases him roughly and storms back over to
Gatekeeper.)*

HAMLET
Good GOD!

HAMLET SR.
Lust? Really?

HAMLET SR. steps into red area.

HAMLET SR.
You have no lust issues with me, Son?

HAMLET
(Hands him a knotted rope) Not that I know of.

HAMLET SR.
You sure?

HAMLET
(Creeped out—untangling the rope.) Unless—

HAMLET SR.
Yes?

HAMLET
I suppose if you'd lusted after my mother more, she wouldn't have—

HAMLET SR.
Oh, right. Blame the victim.

HAMLET
See, I don't know how to do this—

HAMLET SR.
Your mother didn't cheat on me, Son.

HAMLET
But she lusted after—

                HAMLET SR. gives him a hard look.

HAMLET
Got it. *(To Gatekeeper)*
Moving on?

>*Existential pause.*

ROSENCRANTZ
Well, that wasn't so hard.

POLONIUS
(To Gatekeeper) May we—

GATEKEEPER
You may.

>*Orange light rises.*

SCENE 3

GATEKEEPER
(Bangs gavel) Gluttony!

> *HAMLET SR. looks purposefully at Hamlet.*

HAMLET
Um… I don't think so.
You weren't a big eater, except at Twelfth Night—but who wasn't?
You weren't a drunk, and you didn't over-indulge in creature comforts.

HAMLET SR.
Carrying on—

> *All murmur and shift around, creating a second level.*

POLONIUS
(To Hamlet) If I may.
You over-indulged your inclination to make fun of your elders.

GERTRUDE
Indeed, Hamlet.
And you were a glutton for punishment of all kinds, and in all directions.

> *Hamlet sighs and hangs his head.*

CLAUDIUS
You were the product of your upbringing, Hamlet. Now—

HAMLET
(Turns to him with disdain) Yes?
GATEKEEPER
Until you make peace with your uncle's drastically lustful conduct,
you cannot move through Gluttony and on to Avarice.

GERTRUDE
(Suddenly laughing, to Ophelia, referencing Hamlet) Look at him!

OPHELIA
(To Gertrude) Lord of the Manor.

GERTRUDE
(To Ophelia) King of all he surveys.

HAMLET
(To Laertes) Um…

           Gertrude and Ophelia erupt in giggles.

OPHELIA
Yeah.
(To Gertrude) I thought he was taller.

GERTRUDE
Ah, Purgatory.

OPHELIA
The great equalizer.

GERTRUDE
Like a big block of cheese.

OPHELIA
Stops up the pauper AND the prince.

           Gertrude and Ophelia laugh hysterically.

HAMLET
My God, those two are terrifying.

(Shakes his head, then to Claudius) Ugh. Very well.
I've been well rebuked for my own indecency.

CLAUDIUS
Deepest gratitude, sir.
(Starts crossing to the others when HAMLET hits him in the behind with something, knocking him down.)

HAMLET
Wait!

CLAUDIUS
(From the ground) Yes?

HAMLET
You were a glutton for my mother.

CLAUDIUS
Guilty.

HAMLET
You hogged all of her free time.

GERTRUDE
(To Hamlet) What did YOU care?!

HAMLET
I—

CLAUDIUS
It's true. I couldn't get enough of her.
You are her offspring.
(Glances toward Gertrude) I don't believe you can appreciate her deliciousness.

GERTRUDE
(Embarrassed) Would you PLEASE—

HAMLET
Move along, Uncle—unless you have gluttony issues with me?

CLAUDIUS
Well… your appetite for revenge was rather acute.
You stabbed, punched, kicked and poisoned me.

HAMLET
And you blame ME?
CLAUDIUS
(Sighs, hands Hamlet a teapot) Hardly.

GERTRUDE
Onward!

HAMLET SR.
My queen—

GATEKEEPER
No queens in Purga—

HAMLET SR.
Gertrude.

GERTRUDE
Yes?
HAMLET SR.
You indulged in gluttonous consumption of honey wine.

> *HAMLET looks mortified. OPHELIA is*
> *embarrassed for GERTRUDE. The others mumble*
> *and shuffle around, trying to look busy.*

GERTRUDE
Oh! You DASTARD!

HAMLET SR.
(To Gertrude) No man wants to cuddle with a souse.

GERTRUDE
What would you have had me do?!

CLAUDIUS
I enjoyed our boozy tumbles—

GERTRUDE, HAMLET, and HAMLET SR.
Shut UP!

CLAUDIUS
So sorry—

HAMLET
Mother, you did ingest a bucket each day—

GERTRUDE
Honey wine was our joy and our comfort
as we drudged through season after season,
expected to do nothing but look pretty and stitch our lives away—

HAMLET SR.
As did your mother before you—

GERTRUDE
Yes!

HAMLET SR.
Yes—

OPHELIA
(Vehemently) And you're perpetuating the sins of your fathers!

HAMLET SR.
(Pause, a bit nonplussed, then to Gertrude.) You were gluttonous with drink.
That's all I'm saying.

GERTRUDE
FINE!!! I was a SOT!
Happy now?!
(To Hamlet) Satisfied?!

HAMLET
That explains a lot.

GERTRUDE
Oh, good! Blame your inky moods on me.
It's always the mother's fault!

HAMLET
I would rather have been with you, Mother, than with others, when I
was a boy.

GERTRUDE
(Wild, irrational)
When were you ever NOT a boy?!
If you were a man, you could have ended all our miseries long before—

CLAUDIUS
Had you been contented, you would never have been my queen.

HAMLET SR.
Well, isn't that nice?

GERTRUDE

(To Gatekeeper) I admit it! Once I'd risen from my childbed, I drank myself to painlessness every day.

I was a glutton.

A sloppy, sleepy toss-pot!

Can we get on with it, then??

> *Yellow light rises.*

> *Gatekeeper picks up the gavel and points in the direction of the portal to heaven.*

SCENE 4

GATEKEEPER
(Bangs gavel) AVARICE!

LAERTES
Avarice, it is!

> *They all move up a level and hand up to each other all the things again.*
> *The items become the steps, so there are fewer and fewer objects with every level.*
> *They work as they engage in the scene.*

HAMLET
I suppose we should define the term.

POLONIUS
(Pulls a dictionary out of the pile) Latin: *avaritia*, also known as avarice, cupidity, or covetousness. Excessive or rapacious desire, especially for wealth or possessions. See GREED.

HAMLET
(To HAMLET SR.) You were generous with your subjects.
Denmark thrived when you were king.
So excellent a king.

HAMLET SR.
Thank you, son.

> *Pregnant pause.*

HAMLET
(Looks at the rest of the crowd) I don't know, but—we were all well born, at

least, and... maybe greedy for power?
But he just said, "wealth or possessions," so—

LAERTES
Yeah... No.

HAMLET
I'm not feeling it.

GUILDENSTERN
Okay, then!

ROSENCRANTZ
This is a cake walk.

GERTRUDE
Easy for you to say.

> *Green light rises.*
>
> *All scurry up to the next level they have created, handing each other things, hoisting things up, sticking things in crannies to make a stable, relatively level stair.*
>
> *They're bathed in green light.*
>
> *Hamlet is the last one up. He starts to climb up, then stops and takes a step back.*

SCENE 5

LAERTES
We all look like toads.
(Shows his hands to Ophelia) Look at that!

OPHELIA
Dreadful.

GATEKEEPER
(Bangs gavel) Sloth!
Definition?

All reveling in each other's ghastliness.

POLONIUS
(Reading from his dictionary) Any of several slow-moving, arboreal,
edentates of the family Bradypodidae, having a long, coarse,
grayish-brown coat often of a greenish cast caused by algae, and long,
hook like claws used in gripping tree branches while hanging or moving
along in an habitual upside-down position.

LAERTES
Odd.

ROSENCRANTZ
(Nods) Arboreal.

GUILDENSTERN
Fellas—

OPHELIA
(To Polonius) Father—

CLAUDIUS
Unfathomable.

LAERTES
(To Polonius) Perhaps—

ROSENCRANTZ
(To Polonius) Look again.

POLONIUS
Ah. I see.
"Habitual disinclination to exertion;
See LAZINESS."

HAMLET
There we go.

GERTRUDE
Lazy, you were not.
Quite the opposite.

> *Everyone looks at Hamlet intently. Hamlet looks back at everyone.*

OPHELIA
You might well have relaxed a bit more.

CLAUDIUS
You WERE a galvanic youth.

LAERTES
Excitable—

GUILDENSTERN
Lively.

ROSENCRANTZ
Energetic.

GERTRUDE
Vigorous is what you were.

HAMLET
Who among you did I find "lazy"... ???
(Pause—he considers.) Mother, I think you might have—

GERTRUDE
Oh, really?

HAMLET
On second thought—

GERTRUDE
Because if we're going there—

HAMLET
No, see—I can't be intimidated.
I can't lie, none of us can, if we're to get out of here,
(To Gatekeeper) right?
(To Gertrude) I can't pretend, not even to avoid hurting your feelings.

GERTRUDE
How fun for you.

HAMLET
Mother, you were lazy.
You didn't fight for me.

GERTRUDE
Fight for you?

HAMLET
You didn't insist on rearing me yourself.

GERTRUDE
I was a queen!

HAMLET
And you complained all my life

about how dull your life was
and how unsatisfying you came to find your needle projects.

GERTRUDE
I didn't have the faintest idea—

HAMLET
Oh, Mother, please!
As if there weren't a hundred nurses closer than you could throw an
embroidery hoop.
Any number of them could have guided you.
You didn't care!

GERTRUDE
I did care! I just didn't—

HAMLET
What? You didn't WHAT??

GERTRUDE
Queens didn't DO that. I was afraid—

HAMLET
"Oh, frailty, thy name is woman."

OPHELIA
(Throws a hairbrush at him) Oh, what a putrid pile of BOVINE
MANURE!
What was demanded of us, if not frailty? What were we born for, bred
for?
When were we ever encouraged to be strong or brave or courageous?
From birth we were trained to look pretty, smell good and generate
tapestries, tablecloths and handkerchiefs.
You have a helluva nerve.
She was afraid, and that's a female thing? Please.
What was it, if not cowardice, that kept you from making up your mind
to do ANYTHING???

HAMLET
I—

GERTRUDE
You—

OPHELIA
Coward!

HAMLET
Okay, but I wasn't LAZY!

OPHELIA
Neither was your mother.
Fear is not one of the deadly sins.

HAMLET
Well, it should be.

OPHELIA
Then we'd all be dead.
Or worse off… or something.
But, while we're on the subject of sloth and laziness—
(To Polonius) I've got a bone to pick with you.

POLONIUS
Moi??

OPHELIA
I HAD NO MOTHER.
My mother died when I was born,
and my mother's nurse—MY nurse—died when I was FOUR.
The one who took her place tortured me. And you didn't care.

POLONIUS
I didn't know!

OPHELIA
I ran to you. I told you!

POLONIUS
I thought you were being dramatic—

OPHELIA
I was a baby.
You'll never know the things she did to me.

POLONIUS
It was such a long time ago—

OPHELIA
I thought I was ugly.
I thought if you genuinely knew me, you'd find me disgusting.
I felt I deserved to suffer.
I hated eating, because when I did, after a few hours, I'd have to use a
chamber pot.
The maid would come in behind me to empty it,
and the nurse made her SAVE IT for the next day —
to rub in my face.
To rub in my face the filth my body produced.

All the men recoil. Cover ears. Look away.

POLONIUS
Daughter, NO!

OPHELIA
Yes.
So I rarely ate.
But when I did, I snuck away and squatted where the pigs fed,
so there'd be no trace.
I became obsessed with water.
I always kept some to clean myself when no one was looking.

GERTRUDE
Yes. Sweet maid.

OPHELIA
I loved to work in the garden,
but the nurse scrubbed under my fingernails until they were raw.
I hated having my hair brushed.
I begged them to keep my hair braided so it wouldn't snarl.
But I was too young to wear it up —
and only commoners kept their hair plaited all the time.
So I endured having my head yanked this way and that,
with no care for my tears.
And everyone said my hair was glorious.
I paid too high a price for it.

HAMLET
I loved the smell of your hair.

OPHELIA
(Throws something at him) You knew nothing of me or my hair! *(She turns on Polonius. Starts throwing more things—clothes, cloth, whatever.)* Why didn't you protect me?!

POLONIUS
My dear girl—

OPHELIA
WHY DIDN'T YOU CARE?!

POLONIUS
(Explodes, without thinking) You killed your mother!

> *Gasps. Silence. Everyone stares at him. Ophelia freezes. Her hands drop.*

LAERTES
(Cold, furious) It was your seed that killed our mother.

POLONIUS
(Weeping) Yes. Yes!

Silence. The emotional air is scorched.

GATEKEEPER
(To Ophelia) Can you forgive him?

OPHELIA
(Pause. Shocked. Honest.) Yes.
(Pause) I pity him.

POLONIUS
(Wiping his face) Yes. I am pitiful.

Everyone slowly starts to move again. Breath returns.

HAMLET
(To HAMLET SR., softly) Yeesh. Your visage is ghastly.
You don't belong here.
 You were the antithesis of lazy.
 I marveled at your energy and strength.

ROSENCRANTZ
This really isn't so bad at all, is it?

GUILDENSTERN
Not at all.
If this keeps up, we'll sup in Heaven.

Blue light rises.

SCENE 6

GATEKEEPER
(Bangs gavel) WRATH!

HAMLET SR.
(Creates a step up to the next level) Wrath.

GUILDENSTERN
What's this one?

ROSENCRANTZ
Wrath.

OPHELIA
I was never mad at anyone—not until it was far too late.

HAMLET
I was full of wrath.

GERTRUDE
Indeed, you were.
It drove you to break the commandment—you certainly did not honor
me…

> *Gertrude smacks Hamlet, who falls against*
> *Rosencrantz.*

ROSENCRANTZ
…you had me killed—

GUILDENSTERN
(Nods) And me.

POLONIUS
And out of anger at your uncle you carelessly stabbed me—

OPHELIA
You took from me my father—

CLAUDIUS
You killed me twice.

HAMLET
You had it coming.

CLAUDIUS
I did. Still—

OPHELIA
Had you not been wrathful—

GERTRUDE
Perhaps we'd be playing with our great-grand babes today—

HAMLET
(Holds up a nondescript piece of cloth) Instead of sifting through this rubbish.

GATEKEEPER
You're rehashing—Right?!

HAMLET
Right?!

GATEKEEPER
If you're going to rehash, it better end in blood or breakthrough.

CLAUDIUS
May I suggest—

HAMLET
You had plenty of wrath, Uncle.
You ordered my assassination.

CLAUDIUS
Yes—

GUILDENSTERN
Which led to—

ROSENCRANTZ
Our ultimate demise...

HAMLET
I thought you had conspired with him *(points at Claudius)* to have ME killed!

ROSENCRANTZ
But you were wrong!

GUILDENSTERN
We didn't!

HAMLET
I was mistaken—

CLAUDIUS
But I got the ball rolling. I'm to blame for all of it.

GERTRUDE
Oh, stop reveling in your contrition. It's revolting.

CLAUDIUS
I do apologize—

GERTRUDE & HAMLET
Shut UP!

CLAUDIUS
Sorry.

GERTRUDE
UGH!

HAMLET
Mother.

GERTRUDE
What?!

HAMLET
You seem pretty... well... angry.

GERTRUDE
Damn right, I'm angry!

HAMLET
Well... I have issues with that.

GERTRUDE & OPHELIA
Too bad!

OPHELIA
This is Purgatory, pal. All bets are off.

CLAUDIUS
Women aren't allowed to be angry when they're alive, are they?

POLONIUS
Heavens, no!

ROSENCRANTZ
Angry women?!

POLONIUS
Horrors!

GUILDENSTERN
Yuck!

GERTRUDE
(Throws up her hand—all the men flinch) Enough!

OPHELIA
Where were we?

GATEKEEPER
PEOPLE!
Look deeper. You want Heaven? Dig for it.
Look deeply into the bottom of your souls!

LAERTES
(To Gatekeeper) You're beautiful when you're angry.

Gatekeeper gives him an incredulous dismissal.

GUILDENSTERN
 I don't think—

GATEKEEPER
(To all but Claudius) Are you really going to tell me that you forgive this
rogue?
(To HAMLET SR.) After he poured poison in your ears so that he could
have your queen and your crown?!

HAMLET SR.
Well, there's no point—

GUILDENSTERN
(Startlingly angry) He disintegrated your insides, man!

HAMLET SR.
He did, but he's apologized—

POLONIUS
(To Claudius) A simple apology does seem a BIT tame—

LAERTES
You KILLED THE KING!

CLAUDIUS
I did, and I SAID I WAS SORRY—

POLONIUS
(To Gatekeeper) For that he gets to go to Heaven?

OPHELIA
Really?!

POLONIUS
Did it occur to you that there'd be a chain reaction?
That more than just your brother would suffer?
It never occurred to you that Hamlet might go mad?

GERTRUDE
(To Claudius) Did it not occur to you that he'd blame ME?

HAMLET
I didn't exactly BLAME you—

GERTRUDE
You said your father had "Hyperion's curls, the front of Jove himself,"
and said your uncle was a mildewed EAR! —
as if there's any accounting for taste.
But, confound it, *(to Claudius)* you cared more about saving your own
skin than stopping me from drinking that reeking poisoned wine!
Can't you imagine how badly that stung!?

CLAUDIUS
Oh, my love—

GERTRUDE
(Smacks him) DON'T "my love" ME!

HAMLET
(To Claudius) I really should have killed you when I had the chance—

CLAUDIUS
(Confused) When you had the chance?

HAMLET
When you were at prayer after the play.

CLAUDIUS
You could have killed me?

HAMLET
Yes.
You were on your knees alone and praying. No guards.
I stood behind you, dagger drawn and ready to drive it into your skull,
when I realized that if I did, I'd send you straight to Heaven.
So I waited, to make sure you'd go to Hell.

GUILDENSTERN
(Suddenly furious) The Devil take you, then!
It wasn't enough for you to be the prince of Denmark —
you fancied yourself GOD of the universe!
You made it your personal quest to damn us all to HELL!

ROSENCRANTZ
Easy—

GUILDENSTERN
(To Rosencrantz) Are you stupid, you marble-brained sycophant?!
He made sure that we had all our sins on our heads when we died, didn't
he?!

ROSENCRANTZ
(To Hamlet) Did you?!

HAMLET
I— (hesitates)

GATEKEEPER
Spill it!

HAMLET
Well, you were taking a letter to England calling for ME to be killed,
why shouldn't I—

GUILDENSTERN
Why shouldn't you??
Maybe because we had NOTHING TO DO WITH IT?!!

HAMLET (Furious)
 And just how the hell was I supposed to know that?!
(Turning on everyone) In life, not ONE of you was honest with me.
I couldn't count on a SINGLE ONE of you to be straight with me.
My uncle was the WORST, but my mother and—
(indicating Polonius) —the old man snuck around and tried to get me to
disclose my heart without just coming out and ASKING ME,
(indicating Rosencrantz & Guildenstern) you couldn't just tell me the truth,
that you were sent for to find out what distempered me.
(To Ophelia) You knew those two measles were listening while we spoke
in the hall—
 you couldn't have whispered in my ear? Given me a little heads up?!

GUILDENSTERN
(Completely loses it) It's always everyone else's fault, isn't it?!
You had it all, but it wasn't enough, was it, you lousy, moaning spawn of
Lucifer!
(To Gertrude) You coddled him,
(To HAMLET SR.) you overindulged him,
(To Claudius) you competed with him,
(To Polonius) you cowered before him,

(To Ophelia) you worshipped him,
(To Rosencrantz) and YOU!

ROSENCRANTZ
What did I do that you didn't do??

GATEKEEPER
If you don't forgive him—

GUILDENSTERN
FORGIVE HIM?!
I'll burn in hell first!

LAERTES
(In Hamlet's face) You stabbed through the curtain without a thought,
without a breath,
you STABBED MY FATHER and killed him dead.

HAMLET
Well, he was eavesdropping.

LAERTES
Oh, no! Eavesdropping! Off with his head!

HAMLET
I have apologized—

POLONIUS
He has.

LAERTES
You killed my entire family!

HAMLET
Hit me.

LAERTES
(Turns toward Hamlet) Huh??

HAMLET
Go ahead, hit me.
Hit me in the face.

LAERTES
That doesn't work.

HAMLET
Why not?

LAERTES
I killed you once, we even made peace,
and here I am all balled up with anger again,
just talking about it.

OPHELIA
HIT HIM!!

>*Characters all start yelling at each other. Guildenstern*
>*gets knocked out.*
>*They're all literally at each other's throats and have one*
>*another by the hair—a fun bit of choreography.*
>*All screaming insults and accusations—until*
>*Gatekeeper cuts them off.*

GATEKEEPER
(Blows a whistle) KNOCK IT OFF!

>*All stop and look at Gatekeeper. She picks up different*
>*pieces of the pile and thrusts them at everyone.*

GATEKEEPER
Are you all insane?!
This is it. Your last stop. One more step and it's not light you're climbing
into—it's fire.

ROSENCRANTZ crouches by
GUILDENSTERN and tends to him.

ROSENCRANTZ
He was always a good friend.
A gentle man.
(Looks at Hamlet) You've broken him.

HAMLET
Me?!
How did I—

OPHELIA
You had him killed, you droning lout!
You meant for him to burn in HELL!

GATEKEEPER
(Blood boiling) You have a choice. Right now. This is it.
Either you all agree to go forward and work your way out of this,
or stop now and all go downstairs.

ROSENCRANTZ
Well, I'm not forgiving him—look at this!

LAERTES
(To Hamlet) What you did to my sister!

POLONIUS
(To Hamlet) What you did to ME!

HAMLET SR.
(To Claudius) What you did to my QUEEN!

CLAUDIUS
What YOU did to your queen!

GERTRUDE
But, what I did.
(Pause) What I did.
What I didn't do.
(To Gatekeeper) You said we're all one.
(Pause) I feel no forgiveness toward the Old King.
I hate and resent him.
I feel no kinship with him, not even through my son.
(She shrugs, defeated) How can I forgive, when my heart is stone?

GATEKEEPER
You are damned.
You are all DAMNED.
(Crosses to the red portal) Let's go.

> *(Thunder rumbles, the cyc is blood red. Ominous music rises.)*

> *(OPTIONAL INTERMISSION.)*

GATEKEEPER
Come on, get moving!
All of you!
Downstairs!

> *All are stricken with the gravity of the moment. Ophelia looks at Polonius, crosses to him, puts her arms around him.*

OPHELIA
Not him!

LAERTES
(Puts his arms around Ophelia) Not her!

> *The rest of these lines overlap, a cascade as they all physically connect with eachother:*

88

ROSENCRANTZ
Not him, by GOD!

POLONIUS
He has done NOTHING—

GERTRUDE
Oh, please—

CLAUDIUS
My brother—

HAMLET SR.
(Reaching toward Hamlet) Spare him—

GERTRUDE
Not him—

ROSENCRANTZ
Guildenstern—

LAERTES
My sister—

GERTRUDE
My son—

HAMLET SR.
Please—

> *They all cling to each other. Hamlet turns, sees the chain*
> *they've become.*

HAMLET
(Pause)
Look at us.

GATEKEEPER
Get over here!

They continue to cling to each other, huddling closer still.
Gatekeeper watches them stoically.

GATEKEEPER
As it is, this portal will be your last.
You will not ascend!
You're a tangle of egos, soaked in blood and too proud to kneel.

OPHELIA
(Grabs hold of Polonius' hand and Hamlet's, creating a closed circle with herself
facing outward, toward Gatekeeper) For pity's sake, lady! Mercy.
I beg you, MERCY!

CLAUDIUS
This is all my fault.

ALL EXCEPT CLAUDIUS
SHUT UP!!!

OPHELIA
(Breaks loose, throws herself at Gatekeeper's feet) Please, lady. PLEASE!

GATEKEEPER
It's too late.

OPHELIA
(Weeping) Madame, I pray you!
I beg you, implore you!
Give us another chance!

GATEKEEPER
It's not UP TO ME, you little fool!
Don't you see that??
This is MY purgatory, too.

I have to watch you idiots come in here and fight your petty wars
and half the time be condemned because you don't have the courage to
look at YOUR complicity
and to forgive each other.
It's just STUPID!
Have you all forgotten your prayers?!
You were given instructions;
before you could feed yourselves, you were told exactly what to do
to avoid the flames and ascend to paradise, but you're too busy
squabbling to humble yourselves.
Morons.

> *Ophelia suddenly understands. She falls to her knees,*
> *makes the sign of the cross, and begins to pray. The*
> *others, each at their own pace, fall to their knees, cross*
> *themselves, and say the Act of Contrition—some in*
> *Latin, some in English.*

> *Lighting changes in some mysterious way*

ALL (except Gatekeeper and unconscious Guildenstern)
Deus meus, ex toto corde pænitet me omnium meorum peccatorum,
eaque detestor, quia peccando, non solum pœnas a te iuste statutas
promeritus sum, sed præsertim quia offendi te, summum bonum, ac
dignum qui super omnia diligaris. Ideo firmiter propono, adiuvante
gratia tua, de cetero me non peccaturum peccandique occasiones
proximas fugiturum. Amen.

ENGLISH VERSION (simultaneously spoken)
O my God, I am heartily sorry for having offended thee.
And I detest all my sins because of thy just punishments,
but most of all because they offend thee, my God,
who art all good and deserving of all my love.
I firmly resolve, with the help of thy Grace,
to sin no more and to avoid the near occasion of sin.
Amen.

They all cross themselves again when they finish the prayer. Silence. The "phone" rings again. Gatekeeper answers it.

GATEKEEPER
(Into mouthpiece) Yes?
(Listens, then responds) Very good, your grace.
Would there be something more, your grace?
(Pause, then she puts down the ear and mouthpieces, glares at everyone.)
You have been reprieved.

Lighting restores.

OPHELIA
(Throws her arms around Gatekeeper) Oh, thank you! THANK YOU, MADAME!!!

GATEKEEPER
(Tries not to smile) Don't thank me.
Left to my own devices I'd chuck you all in the furnace.
(To all) Now, back to work!

LAERTES
(Crosses with seething anger to a section of the pile that gets his attention)
Let Hercules himself do what he may, the cat will mew and dog will have his day.

Hamlet finds a broken bench. He and Laertes get to work fixing it.

HAMLET
Okay…

LAERTES
MAN, could you turn a phrase. I—

Dammit, man!
Wasn't it just a MINUTE ago you were flirting with my sister
and I was at school and—

HAMLET
It all happened so fast—
If your father hadn't—
If my UNCLE hadn't—

LAERTES
But then your mother—

HAMLET
And then your FATHER—
But, ultimately—

HAMLET & LAERTES
Me.
(Look at each other, amazed) You?!
(More confused) WHY?!

LAERTES
I wanted to cut your throat i' th' church!

HAMLET
For good reason!
I killed your father and drove your sister to suicide!

LAERTES
She fell asleep—

HAMLET
Singing with the fairies.
She'd gone 'round the bend!

LAERTES
She was always extra fragile.

HAMLET
And I—

LAERTES
Before I left, I told her you were trifling with her—

HAMLET
I should have asked her—

LAERTES
She was too young—

HAMLET
That's what I thought!

LAERTES
But you wanted to—

HAMLET
 I did.

POLONIUS
(Steps in) It's all my fault.
I underestimated you, Hamlet.

HAMLET
You were her father! You did what—

LAERTES
We underestimated HER.

POLONIUS
We did.

LAERTES
She was beautiful,
but we didn't think she was bright enough to keep up with you, Hamlet.

HAMLET
I played games with her.

POLONIUS
That is the way of love—

HAMLET / LAERTES / POLONIUS
This is all MY fault.
(They look at each other) I HATE MYSELF!

> *The bench is fixed. Polonius plops down in the middle.*
> *Hamlet and Laertes sit on either side of him. Gertrude*
> *hands them a thick rope pulley system that's tangled.*
> *They all work on untangling it.*
>
> *Gertrude makes a rope out of sheets.*

GERTRUDE
Ah, there's the rub.

OPHELIA
You blame yourselves—

GATEKEEPER
You hate yourselves—

GERTRUDE
You feel just terrible about everything—

OPHELIA
You apologize all over yourselves—

GATEKEEPER
Then turn 'round and do it again.

GERTRUDE
Always.

OPHELIA
All the same things—

GATEKEEPER
All the time.

GERTRUDE
It's not you,
it's not your fathers
any more than it's your mothers and their fathers and mothers before
them.
We are Eve and Adam.
We had Eden, and we blew it.
All we needed was in our reach,
but we just HAD to eat the apple.
We had to control, conquer and second-guess creation.

GATEKEEPER
Going all the way back to the first time human beings decided to harvest
seeds,
organize and plant crops—that was it, the fall from Grace.

OPHELIA
We didn't trust PERFECTION.

GATEKEEPER
It's not human nature to be content, is it?

GERTRUDE
We, who bear the babies, tend to carry the water and make the meals.
You, who sire them, tend to carry the spears and bring the meat.
Still, we've done our share of the heavy lifting —
and you have sung your share of lullabies.
We built the fire.
You carried the kill.
And somehow, we both froze.

Thoughtful silence.

GATEKEEPER
Something about controlling the seed—
planting in neat rows and harvesting and grinding with sharp edges—
something about that doesn't sit well with Grace.

OPHELIA
Thus, we fell,
and thus, we've been at each other's throats ever since.

GERTRUDE
If we want to look at this microcosmically,
it all goes back to your father, Hamlet.
He was a bad husband and a great father.
Had he been a great husband and a bad father,
I'd wager your uncle wouldn't have followed the path to cataclysm,
and had he not, your father wouldn't be murdered,
nor would he have charged you to avenge his death,
nor would be dead the good old man *(gestures toward Polonius)*
his daughter *(gestures toward Ophelia)*
his son *(gestures toward Laertes)*
your schoolmates *(gestures toward Rosencrantz and Guildenstern)*
your uncle, you or I.

HAMLET SR.
I wasn't such a great father.

HAMLET
You WERE!

HAMLET SR.
Nay.
My mind and heart were elsewhere.
I had subjects and lands, dominions to rule and conquer.

HAMLET
(Humiliated) I wish we could start again.

POLONIUS
If wishes were fishes, we'd all cast nets in the sea.

> *Big, awkward silence. The pulley thing is untangled.*
> *Gertrude's rope is done.*
> *She ties one end to the bench, the other to the platform.*
>
> *Violet light slowly starts rising up one level.*

HAMLET
(Fixing a big hook from the pulley onto the back of the bench) These revelations do wear one down.

POLONIUS
Like waves on the rocks at Cyprus.

OPHELIA
Come along, papa—have a look at the pretty purple light.

> *They climb up into the violet.*

GERTRUDE
(Gestures to everyone to HEAVE HO! The bench, with Hamlet and Laertes on it, is hoisted to the violet level.) With a hey and a ho and a HEY, nonny—

GUILDENSTERN
(Waking from a nightmare. Rubs his face, looks around, embarrassed.) No!

ROSENCRANTZ
(Thrilled) My most favored friend!
(Helps Guildenstern up) You missed the fulminations.

GUILDENSTERN
(As R&G clamber up) I dreamed I was planting rye, on my knees,

from a little pouch on my belt.
My back was killing me.

All settle into the violet light, except HAMLET SR.

HAMLET
(Looking at everyone in the violet light) Whew. Better.

HAMLET SR.
Better?

HAMLET
Easier on the eyes. *(He starts climbing up)*

GATEKEEPER
(To Hamlet) NOT so fast!

> *Maybe she has a really long hook and pulls him back
> down. He is unsteady on his feet, then rights himself and
> is face to face with his father.*

HAMLET SR.
I showed my anger—

HAMLET
You never punished me,
you were never unkind, until—

HAMLET SR.
Until—

HAMLET
I—

HAMLET SR.
Don't hold back, Son.
Get it out!

HAMLET
(Finds a set of knives and leather sheath cloth, arranges them by size) Well, you—

HAMLET SR.
(Finds a pipe and flint/ steel, tries to light it) What?!

HAMLET
Dammit, man, I was just a kid!
You haunted me and told me to avenge your murder!

HAMLET SR.
I didn't think you'd take it literally—

HAMLET
What did you think I would do?
Bore him to death?

HAMLET SR.
Now that you mention it—

HAMLET
Come on!

HAMLET SR.
You're right, Son.
I was wrong.

HAMLET
And that led to all of this—all the rest of it!
Polonius, Ophelia, Rosencrantz and Guildenstern, Mother, Laertes,
Claudius—

HAMLET SR.
Yes, Son.
You have a lot of blood on your hands.
I was stuck down here feeling sorry for myself,
which is why I've been here so long.

Look at me.
I'm a fossil who can't even light a damn pipe! *(Throws the pipe and flint/steel back on the pile, works on making a step)*

HAMLET
What do we do now?

CLAUDIUS
Wanna punch me?

HAMLET
(Hesitates) I don't think so.
(Pause) No. Definitely not.
(to HAMLET SR.) You were—
I... I shall not look upon your like again.

> *Both Hamlets step up to the violet with all the others.*

SCENE 7

Blue light fades completely as violet rises to full.

GATEKEEPER
(bangs gavel) ENVY!

HAMLET
I envied you all my life.
I wanted to be you.

HAMLET SR.
Son.

HAMLET
You didn't envy anyone.
You were king. You were the source and summit of Denmark's glory.
We all envied you.
Please, highness—move on.

HAMLET SR.
Hamlet.
There are no kings here.
Your highness is no more.
Can't you feel that?

HAMLET
(Close to tears) No!
You are my liege, my lord, my king father forever.

HAMLET SR.
I am a soul in Purgatory, son.
With more flaws than you can ever know.
(Pause) Indeed, I did envy.

LAERTES
You, who had it all?

POLONIUS
(Amazed) You envied—

HAMLET SR.
(Assembling the final hoist up to the blue double doors, reluctantly tells the story)
I felt a lot of envy in my life, but most especially—there was a little boy
whose mother came to me for relief.
Her husband had fallen under an ox cart and been killed.
She couldn't pay her rent, so she came to me.
The little boy—couldn't have been older than three—caught my eye,
and there was a spark of recognition between us.
Unlike anything I'd ever known.
First a spark, and then a great fire in my heart.
I looked into his face and there I saw everything pure and precious in
God's infinite universe.
That dear child put his little arms up to me, and I raised him up and held
him.
He put his sweet head against my neck, and I felt as if he belonged there.
His mother cried, so frightened that I'd be offended,
and she pulled him from me, which couldn't have hurt more had she
ripped off my arm.
He giggled into her skirts as I told her to have no fear,
that her rent would be forgiven.
She bowed down low, thanked me, thanked and thanked me,
and then scurried off with her little boy in her arms.
He kept looking over her shoulder and waved goodbye to me until she
had disappeared into the throng.
(Pause) I envied that woman—the mother of that sweet child.
I never forgot him.

A pause, like the silence just before an earthquake.

GERTRUDE
(Hurt to the bone, ANGRY) You envied some PEASANT WOMAN?!

103

HAMLET
(Also hurt) Where was I?

HAMLET SR.
(Deeply emotional, continues working without looking at them)
Off at school.

HAMLET
But—

HAMLET SR.
I can't explain it, Son.
(Pause) I never experienced such a kindred feeling in my life, but for that
brief moment with that tiny child.

> GERTRUDE *and* HAMLET *stack trunks and*
> *boxes to help make the step to the final level.*
> *All others have their eyes on* HAMLET SR.

GERTRUDE
(To Gatekeeper) WHERE IS GOD?!

GATEKEEPER
God is— *(in every atom of everything that exists)*—

GERTRUDE
Come on!
You're the gatekeeper. Tell me!
WHERE IS GOD?!

HAMLET
Mother!

GERTRUDE
(Throwing things, wildly) What kind of a GOD gives to a king a queen and
a prince who adore him,

then turns around and lets him fall in love with some RANDOM
URCHIN?!

OPHELIA
(Crosses to Gertrude, tries to comfort her, but Gertrude shakes her off)
 Oh, lady—

GERTRUDE
What new STINKING MUTTON IS THIS?!

GATEKEEPER
(Climbs up to Gertrude) Madame!
MADAME!!
You must cease and desist—

GERTRUDE
Or WHAT?!

GATEKEEPER
Blasphemy, lady.

GERTRUDE
Blasphemy?! I'll show you blasphemy.
GOD is a cruel, sadistic PIG!

> There is a crack of thunder and several lightning bolts.
> All cower except Gertrude, who screams to the heavens.

GERTRUDE
Yes, thunder, CRACK me to dust!
Lightning, spit your fire!
I never gave you all my heart, my life—you owe me NOTHING!
Here I am, a wretched old hag—your slave!
Go ahead, KNOCK yourself OUT!

HAMLET
Mother, NO!

OPHELIA
Oh, LADY!

GERTRUDE
What do I care?!
I'm an insect.
I AM NOTHING!

GATEKEEPER
No, lady, NO!

LAERTES
Yes.

GERTRUDE
Yes?!

LAERTES
I think we are insects.
Spiders on the ends of strings over flame.

OPHELIA
No, SURELY—

LAERTES
What is the point of ANYTHING?!
(Looks longingly at Gatekeeper) I followed every rule and I died before I
ever had a woman look at me as hers. As home.
(Looks at Ophelia) If we're pure as snow, we can still lose our mother in
childbirth and have a fiendish nurse.
(To Heaven) We can be evil malefactors and die peacefully in our sleep
after making Acts of Contrition!
There is no justice.
There is no order—WHY BOTHER DOING ANYTHING?!
Why live a virtuous life when at any time,
after a moment of weakness wherein you eat a third helping of kidney
pie, some hothead stabs through the arras

and sends you to Purgatory?
DO YOU SEE THIS, OH GOD?!
Yes! You see and you LAUGH!

GATEKEEPER
That ache? It's universal. Now, BACK TO WORK!

GERTRUDE
WHAT WORK?!
Making this vile, fetid staircase??

GATEKEEPER
Working it out with each the other!
There is no time to waste!

GERTRUDE
BUGGERALL!!!! *(Turns and angrily works on a section.)*

HAMLET
Where are we?

ALL (except Hamlet)
Envy.

POLONIUS
Inspired Cain to kill Abel.

HAMLET
Certainly, my uncle envied my father.

CLAUDIUS
I did, indeed.

All eyes on Claudius.

CLAUDIUS
(Hesitantly, but feeling the pressure) Scripture tells us that Eve ate the
forbidden fruit,

gained knowledge of good and evil,
and that was the original sin with which we've all been cursed ever since.
It's not our nature to be content
(To Gatekeeper) —as you said.
But how could we be?
How could we, *(Eyes closed, relishing the memory of sensation)* once we'd
bitten down on that magical fruit —
settle for a handful of oats? *(Opens his eyes, suddenly embarrassed, self-conscious)*

HAMLET
I never liked you.

GERTRUDE
(To Hamlet) Cut it out!

HAMLET
(To Claudius—reviewing, incredulously) I stood over you with a dagger,
Uncle.
As you prayed.

CLAUDIUS
(Weakly) Yes, I know.

HAMLET
I didn't want to send you straight to Heaven.
So I waited, and all these people's deaths are on my soul—

OPHELIA
And if A hadn't happened, B would never have taken place—

ROSENCRANTZ
Without B, there'd be no C—

GUILDENSTERN
Without C, I'd be the envy of every—

HAMLET
I envied my father.
I envied his self-control, his confidence.
I envied him his faith,
which ultimately killed him.

ROSENCRANTZ
I envied your position, Hamlet.
You had it made.

GUILDENSTERN
Well, I didn't.
(Smoldering, to Hamlet) I was just glad to call you my friend.

HAMLET
My shame could build a monument.

LAERTES
Mine could throw a shadow over the great pyramids.

OPHELIA
We get it, guys.
You're ashamed of yourselves.

HAMLET
And you, the fair Ophelia—had you no envy in life?

OPHELIA
Yes. I did.
(To Hamlet, Laertes, Rosencrantz, and Guildenstern) I envied your freedom.
(To Gertrude) I envied your dignity.
(To Claudius) I envied your presence.
When you scowled, Denmark shuddered.
(To Polonius) Father, I—
I don't think I envied you.

POLONIUS
But I envied you, Daughter.
Your grace.
Your sweetness.

OPHELIA
I thought that irritated you—

POLONIUS
Only because I didn't have it—

CLAUDIUS
It was a man thing.

ROSENCRANTZ
Not with me.

GUILDENSTERN
Not with us.

POLONIUS
You were powerless little side-kick types.

ROSENCRANTZ
I suppose…

GUILDENSTERN
(To Polonius) You were an old Pantaloon.

POLONIUS
Ouch.

GUILDENSTERN
No offense.

ROSENCRANTZ
In the spirit of this thing we're doing here—

POLONIUS
No, no. I get it.
In life, I'd obfuscate with pomposity and pretension.
Now that we must lay bare our souls, I want to say something like,
"Yes, I know. I'm a jabbering old fool,"
or whatever it is...
Then, I'd go for sympathy —
"and since my wife died, I've never felt appreciated,"
or "there I was, sad, sloppy drunk, drooling on the bar all alone" —
that means I was grieving, you know—or... whatever.
Something to give the impression that I deserved compassion
and had a handle on things.
I never found a way to share my grief with my son
or to bring up my daughter.
I so wanted to do it wisely and intelligently,
but I willfully pretended I thought I WAS wise and intelligent
and ignored the looks from everywhere
that told me I was a buffoon
and unworthy of such miraculously beautiful children.
That is what I was, you know.
Damn my pathetic—
It's common for us tedious old fools to delude ourselves.
Well, gentlemen, here I am, as ever,
making a bumbling speech....
Thereupon, seeing that the marrow of salvation seems to be shutting the hell up,
I'd best do that.

ROSENCRANTZ
Oh, sir.

GUILDENSTERN
You are delightful.

POLONIUS
You're just saying that.

ROSENCRANTZ
No, sir.
 Really!

GUILDENSTERN
We always got a kick out of you.

ROSENCRANTZ
You made us laugh.

POLONIUS
I know I was the butt of many a joke.

He picks up some rags and folds them.

GUILDENSTERN
You made it easy....

ROSENCRANTZ
Sir, no!
We laughed not AT you—

GUILDENSTERN
We were as powerless as you—

ROSENCRANTZ
And we tried to think of things to say—

GUILDENSTERN
To make us seem relaxed, when—

ROSENCRANTZ
We rarely were—

GUILDENSTERN
Except when we were alone together—

ROSENCRANTZ
Or at the pub with other impotent wretches.

GUILDENSTERN
You know—

ROSENCRANTZ
Misery loves company and all that—

GUILDENSTERN
We would have liked to get to know you better.

POLONIUS
You wouldn't hoodwink an old Pantaloon?

ROSENCRANTZ
Methinks we can't dissemble here.

GATEKEEPER
You can't.
Move along, fellas.

> *Rosencrantz, Guildenstern, and Polonius work together on a section of the next level and pass things to each other to build the final level.*

GERTRUDE
(Devoid of feeling) I envied everyone.
Ophelia—I envied your youth.
I saw in you everything I would never know or do that I had longed—
I wanted you near me because I knew Hamlet loved you,
and I wanted him around me.
I wanted to be grandmother to your children.

OPHELIA
I would have loved that.

I thought I could never be a queen as you were—
so comfortably regal.

GERTRUDE
That was a mask.

CLAUDIUS
I envied you, Hamlet,
because she adored you. Fiercely.

GERTRUDE
I did.
And Hamlet, I never felt that I lived in your esteem.
I wanted to, fiercely.

HAMLET
I loved you, Mother, but—
had my father doted on you,
I'd have taken his lead.
(Vehemently) What an ass I was!

> *Eerie music rises. It is time for all to enter the final
> portal, which they do without discussion.
> A sense of trepidation and humility pervades.
> They carry up the final bits of things to finish up the top
> step.*
>
> *Lavender light rises.*

SCENE 8

HAMLET
Oh, PRIDE!

HAMLET SR.
Yes, Hamlet. Pride.
If ever you loved me.

HAMLET
Oh, God!

HAMLET SR.
Let me have it.

HAMLET
I was the proud one, poor Ghost.

HAMLET SR.
Pity me not!

HAMLET
No, not pity.
We're all ghosts here, as you said.
And we're all one here,
(referring to Gatekeeper) as she said.
And in life, PRIDE was not a sin of yours, Father.
Your most grievous sin was faith. Trust.
Sleeping in the orchard unguarded —
leaving Denmark unattended was your sin.

HAMLET SR.
Yes.
ROSENCRANTZ
(To Hamlet) You demanded absolute loyalty—

GUILDENSTERN
And when you thought it wavered—

LAERTES
Luxuriated in your penchant for sadism.

GERTRUDE
…without entertaining the benefit of the doubt.

OPHELIA
You made fun of me—

GERTRUDE
When she had no recourse—

OPHELIA
…and usually no idea what you were blathering about.

GERTRUDE
Though she wasn't stupid—

CLAUDIUS
I was an arrogant dung beetle.
Agreed?
                              All agree.
HAMLET SR.
Gertrude.

GERTRUDE
(Looks at him) What.
HAMLET SR.
I mistreated you.
I beg your forgiveness.

GERTRUDE
Only because you want to step into Heaven.

HAMLET SR.
What can I do?
What can I say?

GERTRUDE
(Pause) I don't know.
It makes no sense, does it?
Your brother let me drink poison and die a hideous death,
and I still want to spend eternity with him.
He murdered you in the orchard,
and I can't stand the sight of you.

HAMLET SR.
I am grizzled—

GERTRUDE
Oh, please.

HAMLET SR.
You deserved better.
You deserved a worshipful mate who doted on you—

GERTRUDE
Don't patronize me, old man.
I didn't need to be worshipped,
I needed to be LOVED.
I needed to matter to you!
I belonged in your thoughts—

HAMLET SR.
I am a failed husband.
Would that I could go back and change it, but alas—

GERTRUDE
Oh, please. Save it—we both know there's no going back.
(To Gatekeeper) What can I do?

GATEKEEPER
Whatever it takes.

HAMLET SR.
Gertrude—please. Let me fix this.

GERTRUDE
(Laughs bitterly) You're funny.

GATEKEEPER
If you can't forgive him, lady—

GERTRUDE
Oh, all right. I forgive him.
(To HAMLET SR.) Just GO!

GATEKEEPER
Disingenuity doesn't play here.

GERTRUDE
Tell that to HIM!
He does nothing but lie.
HAMLET SR.
Huh?!

GERTRUDE
You lie!
You lied to me every day of our lives.
Every time you looked at me, from the first time you saw me,
you LIED—

HAMLET SR.
Damned if I did!

GERTRUDE
Damned if you didn't!
You—

HAMLET SR.
I never lied to you.
NEVER!

GERTRUDE
You vowed to care for me,
to have and hold and keep me.

HAMLET SR.
I did—

GERTRUDE
You spoke to me the words in the Sarum Rite
and spake them back to you did I,
and I was everything I promised—
bonny and buxom in bed and at board—
though you stopped coming for me once I'd birth'd your son.
HAMLET SR.
Well, I had a lot on my mind.

GERTRUDE
You had one foot out the door
even when you'd just arrived home again,
even after months away.
ou didn't love me, you never even knew me! It was all a big, bloody LIE!

HAMLET SR.
(Thunders) WOMAN!
Desist in your persistent caterwauling—

GERTRUDE
Oh, shut up.
You don't scare me.
What are you gonna do, kill me?!

HAMLET SR.
What do you want from me?!!

GERTRUDE
The truth!

HAMLET SR.
The truth about—

GERTRUDE
About everything!
About me, about us, about our lives and my place in your heart,
which was nowhere.
You'd play such a pretty game in front of the crowds —
your subjects, servants, knights, and my ladies, in front of your son —
you'd bow and kiss the palm of my hand
and pull me close and kiss my brow—

HAMLET
Mother, let him be!
He was KING, not some courtier with time on his hands—

HAMLET SR.
Your mother is right.

HAMLET
Huh?

HAMLET SR.
She's right.
I gave her nothing, save a castle and servants, food and drink—

HAMLET
—And a garden!

HAMLET SR.
 I never—

HAMLET
You had duties far beyond the garden, you had—

HAMLET SR.
I had nothing that mattered more,
nothing that lasts into eternity,
save the two of you,
and I failed you both.

HAMLET
You never failed me!

HAMLET SR.
All I wanted was an heir.
Once you'd survived to maturity,
you were scarcely in my thoughts.

GERTRUDE
 Yes!

HAMLET
NO!

HAMLET SR.
Yes.

> *Gertrude looks at the Gatekeeper, who nods.*

GERTRUDE
(Pause, then honestly) Go, Hamlet.
Go, in the best of health.
I mean it.
Heaven rest you.
(Her burden is lifted.)

> *Gatekeeper rings some kind of bell or chime—maybe a*
> *gong—that signals it's time for a soul to ascend.*

HAMLET
(To HAMLET SR.) Your time is short, methinks.

HAMLET SR.
Yes.

HAMLET
 I don't know how to let go.

HAMLET SR.
Tell me goodbye, Hamlet.

HAMLET
(Struggling) Father, good night.

HAMLET SR.
(Waves to the rest of them) Farewell!

ALL
Goodbye, farewell, etc.

HAMLET SR.
Here I go.
(The upper doors open and he steps through.) Wow...

> *He enters and is engulfed in bright white fog or something. Steps through the portal. Maybe he levitates a bit.*

GERTRUDE
Whew!
That's a relief. *(Laughs)*

LAERTES
Well done, buddy!

HAMLET
Thanks... buddy...

OPHELIA
It's pretty strange, isn't it?
When there's no pecking order.

GERTRUDE
Who are you, if not the prince?

HAMLET
I'm—
I haven't the foggiest.

POLONIUS
Oh, Achilles.

LAERTES
Who knew PRIDE would feel the scariest?

CLAUDIUS
I was spoon-fed pride.
The second son's elixir.
(Turns to Hamlet) My pride could have filled oceans —
I bested your father at swordplay, and he laughed.
He didn't care.
He was first born and would be king
had he no strength to lift a blade.
Still, that was my point of pride until he took his last breath.

OPHELIA
I had no pride at all.

GERTRUDE
That was clear.
You lacked even a hint of arrogance.

OPHELIA
I was afraid to breathe, sometimes.

GUILDENSTERN
I was proud of all the books I had read.

ROSENCRANTZ
(Scoffs) You'd read an *almanac*, in a pinch.
I was proud of my friendship with the prince.
(Deeply embarrassed) God.

LAERTES
I was proud of my father's standing at court
and that I stood in good King Hamlet's regard.
Later *(to Claudius)* yours—
I paid no attention to your dalliance with the queen,
your marriage straight on the heels of the good king's funeral.
I didn't care.

I cared only that my father was a courtier,
and my sister and I grew up at court.
(To Hamlet) I was the ass.

GERTRUDE
I was disgustingly proud.
As a child, a girl, a maid, a princess, a queen —
I felt entitled to and never wanted for a thing in my life,
save your father's attention, Hamlet.
And your favor.

HAMLET
Argh.
I know.
I was—

POLONIUS
I was a proud courtier.
A pompous, self-important fool,
all the more so because my children were beautiful.

> *Everyone pauses, considers, breathes.*

> *Gatekeeper rings the bell/chime/gong seven times. All
> excitedly turn upstage.*

ALL
(Hug each other, kiss, cry) We made it!
At last!
Etc…

SCENE 9

Gertrude hesitates and turns back to Gatekeeper.

GERTRUDE
How do you, lady?

GATEKEEPER
I'm fine.

All hesitate. Gertrude takes a couple of steps toward Gatekeeper.

GATEKEEPER
(Looks up at them, irritated) Go thy ways. Go thy ways! Leave me.

LAERTES
What do you here, lady?

GATEKEEPER
Have no fear. I won't be alone for long.
As soon as you step through the doors, another crop of sinners will arrive.

POLONIUS
This is your afterlife?
Cataloguing lost souls and sending them up and down?

ROSENCRANTZ
When will you depart this grim and disconsolate place?

GATEKEEPER
I don't want to think about it.

ALL exchange looks.

LAERTES
I'm not leaving you here.

GATEKEEPER
Don't be ridiculous!

LAERTES
Come with me, lady—take my hand.

GATEKEEPER
Stop it, now!

GERTRUDE
We can't leave you here! You—

CLAUDIUS
Oh, dear. Are you scheduled to go…
(Pause, looks at the red doors) DOWN?

POLONIUS
Surely not!

GATEKEEPER
(Laughs bitterly) Not too far-fetched.
(Sighs, knowing they'll keep arguing with her. This probably happens a lot) I
choose to be here.

HAMLET
We can wait while you work your way up—

GATEKEEPER
Oh, no.
I must build my own steps to Heaven.

LAERTES
But why all alone?

OPHELIA
We had each other.

GATEKEEPER
As I said, it's my choice.

ROSENCRANTZ
(Making his way down a couple of levels) Well, I'm not leaving without you.

GUILDENSTERN
(Follows Rosencrantz) And I'm not going without him.

GATEKEEPER
That's blackmail!

OPHELIA
(Stepping down) C'est la guerre…

HAMLET
(Getting comfortable) Yep.

GATEKEEPER
Oh, all right!
But if I tell, you must promise to go!

GERTRUDE
No promises.

GATEKEEPER
(Exasperated) Look—I can't leave, because my beloved is stuck.

LAERTES
Damn!

GATEKEEPER
He's walking the Earth as a ghost —
not able to get up here at all.
He doesn't realize he's dead.

ALL
Horrors!

Oh no!
Etc.

GATEKEEPER
All who knew him are long gone,
and he haunts the family tomb.
But there's a groundskeeper who's aware of him, finally.
I'm running on faith, here.

OPHELIA
Oh, lady.
That must have been SOME LOVE you shared.

GATEKEEPER
(Shrugs) We were young. Teenagers.
(Pause) We killed ourselves.

ALL gasp.

Our families were enemies - we married in secret, but he was banishED,
and no one knew... He accidentally killed my cousin, and my mother
wanted him dead. It was ugly. I couldn't bear it - the friar who married
us gave me a potion that made me seem lifeless. He arranged for my
love to come to me, but somehow the wires crossed, and my beloved
thought I was really dead. He went to an apothecary and got lethal
poison, and when he saw me in the tomb, drank the venom and died. I
woke up just then. He was still warm, and I took his dagger and stabbed
myself.

OPHELIA
This is the saddest story I've ever heard in my entire life.
And death.

HAMLET
We thought WE lived a tragic love story.

GATEKEEPER
See?
I can't leave until he can come with me.
At least I have an interesting job.

ALL look at each other with dismay.

LAERTES
But—

GATEKEEPER
GO!

LAERTES
But—

We hear the tortured cries of souls at the door.

GATEKEEPER
No, really.
You're keeping others from coming in.
Get going.

POLONIUS
You are so brave.

LAERTES
(Mournfully) I can't imagine such a love—

GATEKEEPER
Yes, you can.
Just remember what it was like to be an infatuated teenager,
then add an infinite layer of guilt.

POLONIUS
No!

GATEKEEPER
Yes. Now, GO!
(To Hamlet and Ophelia) NOT you!

OPHELIA
WHY?!

GATEKEEPER
You two still have work to do.

> *Laertes reluctantly steps up to the heavenly blue portal.*
> *He steps in, and Polonius, Rosencrantz, and*
> *Guildenstern step into the portal with HAMLET SR.*
> *Claudius takes Gertrude's hand.*

CLAUDIUS
(pauses, turns to Gertrude) Queen of my heart. You saved me. I was damned. Look! *(holds out his hands)* These hands, once stained with my brother's blood are now white as snow. In life, I was starving and thirsty, my ambition never satisfied. Now, all commissions, authority, titles, fallen away. The only crown I wear I share with all of you and all we go to meet. *(Laughs, then to all)* Feel that?

> *They do.*

(Waves) Farewell, Purgatory. I leave you full of remorse and without regret.

> *Gertrude laughs, turns and looks back at HAMLET.*
> *They step through the portal.*

HAMLET
How does my lady for this many a day?

OPHELIA
(Cynically) Well, well, well...

HAMLET
My lady, I have remembrances of yours that I have longED long to
re-deliver— *(Tries to kiss her)*

OPHELIA
(Ducks, crosses away from him) I never gave you aught.

HAMLET
My lady?

OPHELIA
I loved you not.

HAMLET
I was the more deceived.

OPHELIA
(Slaps him, hard) DAMN you!!

HAMLET
(Grabs her, holds her tight) I'll be damned if I can't get us the hell out of
here.

OPHELIA
(Kicks him in the shin) It's not my job to make it easy for you!

HAMLET
(Hopping, holding his shin) Heaven forbid!
Do your worst, lady.
(He falls down) I'll be right here. *(Nurses his shin)*

OPHELIA
You wore your pride like a crown.
I wore nothing.
I was always afraid that you or your mother or someone would notice
that I wasn't actually beautiful.

HAMLET
I loved the smell of your hair.

OPHELIA
That had nothing to do with me.
That was clove, ginger, nutmeg, rose water, and musk.
How I longed to shear it all off
and dunk my head in the stream as you did.
To run, as all you boys did, naked and barefoot in the summer grass.

HAMLET
My lady—

> *Ophelia dissolves, slides to the floor. Hamlet slides close*
> *to her.*

HAMLET
I know it's only an excuse,
but I didn't know—

OPHELIA
You didn't—

HAMLET
No, I didn't care.
I didn't know to care.
I didn't THINK to care.
I had absolutely no idea that you needed or wanted anything at all,
though come to think of it,
you always seemed sad. *(He touches her face)*

OPHELIA
I was all but invisible.

HAMLET
You were so beautiful.
Like Venus.

OPHELIA
And just as irrelevant.

HAMLET
Irrelevant?
She's a goddess!

OPHELIA
She is made of stone.
Her feelings can never be hurt because she doesn't have any.
Put her in a corner for a thousand years,
and she won't mind a bit.

Pause. They muse.

HAMLET
Horatio and I visited the cathedral in Copenhagen when we were
partying there for two straight weeks.
It was his idea, of course. I sure wasn't thinking about church.
But my most excellent of all friends wanted to look at the architecture.
And it was breathtaking.
That night, as we fell asleep, through my mead-soaked haze,
I heard my friend mention that he was surprised there was no statue of
the Lady in the cathedral.
Of course, I hadn't noticed.
But Horatio said he looked for her after a while,
and she was nowhere to be found.
It's the Cathedral of Our Lady of Copenhagen,
and the men that built it left her out.

OPHELIA
(Pause) So, it's not just me.

*Hamlet laughs. She chuckles. Soon they're wrapped in
an embrace, laughing.*
They sit up, wiping tears of laughter away.

OPHELIA
Hamlet.

HAMLET
Yes, m'lady?

OPHELIA
Do you think we'd be us if Eve hadn't eaten that apple?

HAMLET
(Flummoxed) Well—

OPHELIA
I mean, who would we be without the knowledge of good and evil?

HAMLET
I think—

OPHELIA
Can you imagine life without negative and positive?

HAMLET
Well—

OPHELIA
What would it be?

HAMLET
It—

OPHELIA
I mean, it really isn't fair to put all this on Eve, is it?

HAMLET
She—

OPHELIA
Adam ate the apple too, didn't he?

HAMLET
He—

OPHELIA
And, anyway, the flood wiped everything out and we started all over
again with Noah and his family,
and they turned out to be just as corrupt as Adam and Eve's progeny.

HAMLET
Well—

OPHELIA
People are just rotten, don't you think?

HAMLET
(Starts to answer, stops and regroups) Can you forgive me, Lady?
When all is said and done?

OPHELIA
If I cannot forgive you, I cannot forgive Adam.
If I cannot forgive Adam, I must blame God for creating him.
And if I cannot forgive God,
I suppose I have no chance of going with you to Heaven.

HAMLET
Damn.
There's a conundrum.

OPHELIA
Right?

HAMLET
And you can't pretend to forgive God, because—

OPHELIA
Obviously.

HAMLET
So you must actually forgive God.
That feels really weird to say.

OPHELIA
But there it is.
Your mother is with God, and she—

HAMLET
Okay.

OPHELIA
Free will, I think, was the problem.

HAMLET
You are quick, lady.

OPHELIA
How infinite in faculty—

HAMLET
How–
OPHELIA
What if the Holy Spirit is the voice that cries out in the wilderness—
rejecting, despising, and blaspheming?

HAMLET
Wild and whirling words.

OPHELIA
What if the Holy Spirit is the buttress of all, the power of God, the
living life in all that is?

HAMLET
We were taught that we have a magnet within us, a gift from God,
to ward off deception and to motivate us to do good.

OPHELIA
And we're given the power to resist that magnetic force.

HAMLET
I think the Spirit of God is a wild thing.

OPHELIA
Maybe to forgive God is to accept that we're a part of that wildness.

HAMLET
Accept the wild in us.

OPHELIA
What if God is the very heart of Nature?

HAMLET
Then—wildness is sacred.
GOD, but I'm thirsty!

OPHELIA
Oh, me too!

HAMLET
All part of the mystery—

OPHELIA
I think Heaven is running naked and barefoot through fields of wildflowers.

HAMLET
Without all that beautiful hair?

OPHELIA
No tangles in Heaven. Right?
No entanglements of any kind.

Long, flowing hair like silk that never ever needs brushing.
That's what I'd call Heaven.

HAMLET
I can't wait to see!
Do you think we can—

OPHELIA
I think we can. *(Looks at Gatekeeper)*

GATEKEEPER
You can. *(Rings bell/chime/gong.)*

HAMLET
Will we still be us once we leave here?

GATEKEEPER
You won't care.

OPHELIA
I've been wondering that the whole time.
We just have to—

HAMLET
Take a leap of faith—

OPHELIA
I don't have faith, I have… I can't explain it.

HAMLET
Nothing was always my biggest fear.
That the beyond was just—nothing.

GATEKEEPER
It's not nothing.

OPHELIA
It's part of the something, right?
Better than this.

GATEKEEPER
(Chuckles) Better than this.

HAMLET
I want to be with you forever.

OPHELIA
(Guffaws) Oh, BROTHER!

HAMLET
 What?!

OPHELIA
Forever is a LONG time.
Still—I do appreciate it.
If we're one, we're—

HAMLET
Do you think they're all there—where we're going?

OPHELIA
(Standing up, dusting herself off) I hope so.

HAMLET
Our friends and family, all the saints and apostles, and—

OPHELIA
(Extends her hand, helps Hamlet up) I just hope there are PIGS.

> Lights do all kinds of magical things.

> Music rises to a fever pitch as they approach the blue
> doors, hand in hand.

Hamlet looks back and sees Gatekeeper sitting at her desk.

She gives them the thumbs up.

Ophelia disappears into the light.

Hamlet steps forward.

Alone. Silent.

He looks toward the light. We expect a monologue. A soliloquy. An overthink.

He says nothing.

He does nothing.

He's Hamlet. He hesitates.

And then —

Ophelia's hand shoots back through the portal.
She grabs his wrist.
And yanks. Not gently. Not romantically.
Just firm, clean, no choice.

He stumbles forward.

They vanish together.

Gatekeeper shims the desk leg. Stares at it a moment. Looks up, hears the howling again. She sighs. Opens the gate.

Light shift, then fade to black.

END OF PLAY

LEAR
A SOLO ADAPTATION

NOTE FROM THE PLAYWRIGHT

This adaptation takes place in the final flickering moments of Lear's life. Time is no longer linear—his past, present, and hallucinations bleed together as he wrestles with his identity, his legacy, and his failures. The world he once ruled has dissolved; all that remains is himself and his tattered cloak—the last remnant of his kingdom, his power, his madness, and his grief. As he speaks, he relives events as they haunt him.

There are no scene or costume changes, no transition from one physical world to another. The movement is internal—Lear's mind propels him forward, backward, through memory, through delusion, through grief. At the center of this unraveling is the cloak. It is his kingdom, his burden, his madness, his ruin. It is warmth, armor, a banner of authority—until it is not. The way Lear interacts with it shifts as he himself deteriorates. He clutches it for comfort. He wears it as a mantle. He spreads it before him as a kingdom. He throws it away in rage. And, finally, he lets it fall.

The stage directions throughout the script are not blocking notes in the traditional sense. They do not dictate precise physical movement. They are a map of Lear's internal shifts, a guide for the actor to explore how thought, memory, and emotion shape his physicality. They suggest the weight of a moment: when Lear grips the cloak as if testing its reality, it is a reflection of his doubt, his failing grasp on who and what he is. When he lifts it as though presenting the kingdom itself, it is Lear still believing, still trying to make something real that is already gone. Everything the actor does should be in service of this core truth: Lear is living it, reliving it, failing to escape it.

At the end of the piece, there is no resolution. No revelation. No peace. The world does not grant him meaning or comfort. He only loses hold of everything. His voice, his strength, the weight in his arms. And then—nothing.

This is King Lear stripped to its bones. One man. One object. The last breath of a life that has already unraveled.

– Jeanmarie Simpson, March 4, 2025

SCENE I: THE UNRAVELING BEGINS

A dim, fading light. Silence. Not empty, but pressing. A silence thick with waiting, with absence. Then—a breath. Ragged. Shallow. A man, weary and worn, alone. The cloak—once royal—now tattered and filthy—clings to his shoulders. He pulls it tight. A king's mantle. A beggar's rags. A child's comfort.

LEAR

Who is it that can tell me who I am?

The words hang. He waits. Listening. Searching. The silence stretches. It is unbearable.

A pause. The question lingers. He listens, as if waiting for an answer. None comes.

Doth any here know me? This is not Lear.

Doth Lear walk thus? Speak thus? Where are his eyes?

Either his notion weakens, his discernings

Are lethargied—Ha! Waking? 'Tis not so!

He shifts beneath the cloak, fingers pressing into the fabric as if testing its reality—its weight. A flicker of recognition, memory stirring.

Are you our daughter?

What makes that frontlet on? Methinks you

are too much o' late i' th' frown.

He shifts—tries to sit taller. The effort is shaky, unsteady. A grimace. His body is betraying him. For a moment, he sags—but no. Not yet. He forces himself upright, fists tightening in the cloak. A king. Or

something that was one.

Darkness and devils!

Saddle my horses! Call my train together!

Degenerate bastard, I'll not trouble thee;

Yet have I left a daughter.

He reaches into the air—grasping at something that isn't

there. Then, his hand falters. His grip on the cloak

loosens slightly.

Woe that too late repents! O, sir, are you come?

Is it your will? Speak, sir! Prepare my horses!

Ingratitude, thou marble-hearted fiend,

More hideous when thou show'st thee in a child

Than the sea-monster!

To an unseen figure—pleading, furious—he grips the

cloak again, gathering it up in his fists, as though

holding onto some last shred of control.

Detested kite! Thou liest!

My train are men of choice and rarest parts,

That all particulars of duty know

And in the most exact regard support

The worships of their name.

A sharp breath—then a bitter, breathless laugh.

O most small fault,

How ugly didst thou in Cordelia show!

Which, like an engine, wrench'd my frame of nature

From the fix'd place; drew from my heart all love

And added to the gall.

> *His chest heaves. Suddenly, he strikes his own head. The*
> *cloak slips from his grasp, falling in a heap around him.*

O Lear, Lear, Lear!

> *Silence. He stares down. The fabric pools at his feet, but*
> *he makes no move to retrieve it.*

Beat at this gate that let thy folly in

And thy dear judgment out! Go, go, my people.

> *His breathing slows, but his anger still simmers. A long*
> *pause. His hands hover near the cloak, hesitant.*

It may be so, my lord.

Hear, Nature, hear! Dear goddess, hear!

> *Slowly, he reaches down, pulling the cloak back toward*
> *him—not as armor, not as a robe, but as something to*
> *cling to. He gathers it into his lap, fingers gripping it*
> *tightly.*

Suspend thy purpose, if thou didst intend

To make this creature fruitful.

Into her womb convey sterility;

Dry up in her the organs of increase;

And from her derogate body never spring

A babe to honour her!

> *His fingers press into the fabric, his hands tightening as*
> *though wringing the very curse from his body.*

If she must teem,

Create her child of spleen, that it may live

And be a thwart disnatur'd torment to her.

Let it stamp wrinkles in her brow of youth,

With cadent tears fret channels in her cheeks,

Turn all her mother's pains and benefits

To laughter and contempt, that she may feel

How sharper than a serpent's tooth it is

To have a thankless child!

> *A sharp inhale—his shoulders tremble. His arms*
> *instinctively tighten around the cloak, wrapping himself*
> *in it once more. He shivers.*

No, no, they would not!

They durst not do't;

They would not, could not do't.

> *His breath is shaking now. One hand clutches the cloak*
> *against his chest, the other pressing against his heart as*
> *though steadying something inside him.*

O, reason not the need!

Our basest beggars

Are in the poorest thing superfluous.

Allow not nature more than nature needs,

Man's life is cheap as beast's.

His hands tighten again, fingers curling into the fabric.

Thou art a boil,

A plague sore, an embossed carbuncle

In my corrupted blood.

> *A long, slow exhale. His body sags, exhaustion*
> *overtaking him. Then, with one last surge of defiance—*

I will have such revenges on you both

That all the world shall—I will do such things—

What they are yet, I know not; but they shall be

The terrors of the earth!

> *But the fire is already fading. The fight seeps from his*
> *body. His grip on the cloak loosens.*

You think I'll weep.

> *A pause. His breath hitches. He shakes his head, voice*
> *barely above a whisper.*

No, I'll not weep.

I have full cause of weeping, but this heart

Shall break into a hundred thousand flaws

Or ere I'll weep.

> *His body sways. His voice drops to something softer,*
> *pleading—*

O, let me not be mad, not mad, sweet heaven!

Keep me in temper; I would not be mad!

> *His body folds inward. The cloak wraps around him*
> *completely. Silence. The storm inside him has only begun*
> *to rise.*

SCENE II: THE DIVISION OF THE KINGDOM

> *A shift. Lear is no longer the broken man from*
> *before—he is a king. Or he believes himself to be. The*
> *tattered cloak, still filthy, is now draped over his*
> *shoulders, worn like a royal mantle. He clutches at it,*
> *gathering it in his fists as though it were whole—as*
> *though it still carries the weight of his authority.*

Meantime we shall express our darker purpose.

Give me the map there.

> *He lifts a fold of the cloak, spreading it before him as if*
> *unveiling the kingdom itself. His fingers smooth the air,*
> *tracing invisible borders onto the ruined fabric.*

Know that we have divided in three our kingdom,

And 'tis our fast intent to shake all cares and business from our age,

Conferring them on younger strengths, while we

Unburden'd crawl toward death.

> *His hands press the fabric against his chest. A king*
> *holding court—but also a man holding onto something*
> *vanishing.*

Which of you shall we say doth love us most?

That we our largest bounty may extend

Where nature doth with merit challenge.

> *A pause. He waits. The weight of expectation presses*
> *against him.*

Goneril, our eldest-born, speak first.

He listens. Silence. A flicker—doubt? Fear? He
extends a hand, brushing the edge of the cloak as if
marking out her lands.

Of all these bounds, even from this line to this,

With shadowy forests and with champains rich'd,

With plenteous rivers and wide-skirted meads,

We make thee lady. To thine and Albany's issue be this perpetual.

As he speaks, he lifts the cloak slightly—then lets it fall,
as though the gesture alone bestows the land.

What says our second daughter, our dearest Regan, wife to Cornwall?

Speak.

Another pause. He listens. His confidence grows. His
grip on the cloak firms.

To thee and thine hereditary ever

Remain this ample third of our fair kingdom,

No less in space, validity, and pleasure

Than that conferr'd on Goneril.

Now, he turns. His fingers tighten around the fabric,
pulling it close as he calls to the last voice—an absence
heavier than presence.

Now, our joy,

Although the last, not least; to whose young love

The vines of France and milk of Burgundy

Strive to be interest; what can you say to draw

A third more opulent than your sisters? Speak.

A beat. A shadow. The echo of a single word—

Nothing?

His brow furrows. The fabric shifts on his shoulders. He readjusts the cloak, resettling it—as if restoring his authority, as if willing control back into his grasp.

Nothing can come of nothing. Speak again.

But there is no answer. And something in Lear's world begins to crack. His grip on the cloak loosens—suddenly unsure if it is holding him up or weighing him down.

How, how, Cordelia? Mend your speech a little,
Lest it may mar your fortunes.

He leans forward, urging, commanding. But his hands have stilled. The cloak is not royal robes. The fabric does not reassure him.

But goes thy heart with this?

A beat. His voice drops.

So young, and so untender?

Her answer—whatever it was—lands like a blow. He recoils. His hands find the cloak again, but this time they clutch it harder, as if gripping a ruin, as if drowning in it.

Let it be so! Thy truth then be thy dower!

His voice surges—desperate, wounded, furious. And then—

For, by the sacred radiance of the sun,
The mysteries of Hecate and the night;
By all the operation of the orbs
From whom we do exist and cease to be;
Here I disclaim all my paternal care,

Propinquity and property of blood,

And as a stranger to my heart and me

Hold thee from this forever!

> *And then—a violent motion. He rips the cloak from his*
> *shoulders and flings it to the ground. A rejection. A*
> *severing. It lands heavily. His hands still tremble from*
> *the act.*

Peace, Kent!

Come not between the dragon and his wrath.

I lov'd her most, and thought to set my rest

On her kind nursery.

> *He turns away—but the weight of his words staggers*
> *him. His breath hitches. His eyes flicker downward.*
> *The cloak is still there. A thing cast aside—but not*
> *gone.*

Hence and avoid my sight!

So be my grave my peace, as here I give

Her father's heart from her!

> *His voice wavers—he is on the precipice of something he*
> *does not yet understand. His body stiffens. He does not*
> *look down again. He takes a breath—forced,*
> *measured—and turns away from the fallen fabric.*

Call France! Who stirs? Call Burgundy!

Cornwall and Albany,

With my two daughters' dowers digest this third;

Let pride, which she calls plainness, marry her.

He lifts his hands, as though bestowing a crown. But
there is nothing there. The gesture is empty. His fingers
tighten in the air—grasping for something long gone.

I do invest you jointly in my power,

Preeminence, and all the large effects

That troop with majesty.

He straightens—back rigid, forcing the air of a king.
But the cloak lies in a heap at his feet. A king without
a mantle. A father without a child.

Ourself, by monthly course,

With reservation of an hundred knights,

By you to be sustain'd, shall our abode

Make with you by due turns.

Only we still retain

The name, and all th' additions to a king.

The sway, revenue, execution of the rest,

Beloved sons, be yours; which to confirm,

This coronet part betwixt you.

He gestures—bestows—surrenders. But his gaze flickers
back once more. His feet hesitate. The cloak—a thing
he cast off—still lingers.

The bow is bent and drawn; make from the shaft.

A pause. He waits for some feeling of triumph. The
silence presses in. His eyes catch the fabric at his feet.

Nothing! I have sworn; I am firm.

He steps forward, past the cloak, leaving it behind. He does not look back. But the audience sees it. It is still there. The thing he believes he has shed.

SCENE III: THE STORM INSIDE & OUT

*The howling of the wind. Rain, relentless. Thunder
explodes, splitting the sky. Lear staggers forward,
drenched, half-mad. His body is wracked with cold, his
breath ragged. His cloak—his kingdom, his ruin—lies
behind him, abandoned. He turns. Sees it.*

*A flicker of recognition. Then—desperation. He dives
for it. Grabs it.*

*It is too heavy. It drags through the mud. A useless
weight. But still, he pulls it toward himself, clutching it
like a drowning man to driftwood.*

LEAR

Blow, winds, and crack your cheeks! Rage! Blow!

You cataracts and hurricanoes, spout

Till you have drench'd our steeples, drown'd the cocks!

You sulphurous and thought-executing fires,

Vaunt-couriers to oak-cleaving thunderbolts,

Singe my white head!

*He flings the cloak over himself, huddling beneath it—a
desperate shelter, a shield against the storm. He grips it
tight, pulling it around his body, but the wind whips at
the edges, tearing it from his grasp. He fights to hold it
down.*

And thou, all-shaking thunder,

Strike flat the thick rotundity o' the world!

Crack nature's moulds, all germains spill at once,

That makes ingrateful man!

*A sudden burst of thunder. His whole body jerks at the
sound. Then—he throws the cloak open, exposing
himself to the rain, daring the heavens to strike him
down. His laughter erupts—wild, unhinged, lost in the
wind.*

*But his rage does not last. It shifts—searching. His
fingers find the cloak again, digging into the fabric,
twisting it, wringing it like a neck—as if it were the very
daughters who betrayed him.*

Rumble thy bellyful! Spit, fire! Spout, rain!

Nor rain, wind, thunder, fire, are my daughters:

I tax not you, you elements, with unkindness.

I never gave you kingdom, call'd you children,

You owe me no subscription: then let fall

Your horrible pleasure! Here I stand, your slave,

A poor, infirm, weak, and despis'd old man.

*His breath is ragged. His body sinks further beneath the
cloak, clutching at it—but now not as armor. As rags.
As filth. The realization settles over him like the weight
of the storm itself.*

But yet I call you servile ministers,

That will with two pernicious daughters join

Your high-engender'd battles 'gainst a head

So old and white as this. O! O! 'tis foul!

*His legs give out. He collapses completely, curling into
himself, the cloak now a sodden, shapeless heap around*

him. His fury is spent. His body trembles. His
voice—barely a whisper—

I am a man more sinn'd against than sinning.

A moment. Silence. The storm rages, but Lear is still.
He listens, as if waiting for an answer. Nothing. His
hands press into the mud, fingers digging, grounding
himself—or trying to.

Let the great gods,
That keep this dreadful pudder o'er our heads,
Find out their enemies now. Tremble, thou wretch,
That hast within thee undivulgèd crimes,
Unwhipp'd of justice.

His hands find the cloak again. He lifts it, stares at
it—searching it for meaning. Is it his kingdom? His
crown? His very soul? A long silence. Then—

Hide thee, thou bloody hand;
Thou perjur'd, and thou simular man of virtue
That art incestuous. Caitiff, to pieces shake,
That under covert and convenient seeming
Hast practis'd on man's life!

Suddenly—violently— he flings the cloak away. It lands
in a heap, soaked, lifeless. He gasps for air, his chest
heaving. His arms—bare now, exposed— tremble
against the cold. But—he is no freer.

Close pent-up guilts,
Rive your concealing continents, and cry
These dreadful summoners grace!

His hands clutch his head, shaking. The storm rages on.
The cloak—motionless, discarded— is still there. It
does not leave.

My wits begin to turn.

His eyes flicker toward the cloak. A pause. A
hesitation. Some part of him cannot bear to part with it.
His hands hesitate. Then—as if against his own will—
he reaches for it again. He drags it toward himself,
pulling it back around his shoulders, back around his
body. It is heavy, soaked, useless—but he clings to it. A
breath. A whisper—

Come on, my boy. How dost, my boy? Art cold?

His arms wrap around the cloak—not just for warmth,
but as if holding someone close. The Fool? Cordelia?
Himself? He rocks slightly, the motion soothing,
desperate.

I am cold myself.

He buries his face into the fabric. But there is no
warmth there. No comfort. His body sways. He is losing
himself.

Where is this straw, my fellow?
The art of our necessities is strange
That can make vile things precious.

He pulls the cloak tighter—a royal robe? A beggar's
rags? His mind can no longer tell.

Come, your hovel.
Poor fool and knave, I have one part in my heart

160

That's sorry yet for thee.

>He stumbles forward, searching—for shelter, for solace, for something to hold onto. He is failing. He is fading.

O, that way madness lies; let me shun that;
No more of that.

>But even as he says it, something in him knows—it is already too late. His hands press against the cloak, but it is no longer just a garment. It is his ruin. His burden. His past. The wind howls. The fabric in his grip grows heavier.

>He pulls it closer anyway.

SCENE IV: GONERIL & REGAN'S BETRAYAL

*A shift. The storm has quieted, but the cold remains.
Lear stands, shivering, the world around him
indistinct—his daughters' halls, or just the hollow spaces
of his mind? His cloak—dried but still filthy, still
tattered—is clutched around his shoulders, but he is not
huddling beneath it now. He is trying to wear it with
dignity, trying to make it royal again. It hangs unevenly,
twisted between a king's robe and a beggar's rags. He
speaks as if they are before him.*

LEAR

Are you our daughter?

*He smooths the fabric at his chest, as if resetting his
dignity, his authority.*

What makes that frontlet on?

Methinks you are too much o' late i' th' frown.

*He waits for an answer, but none comes. His fingers
twitch at the cloak's frayed edges. A flicker of doubt.
Then, his voice hardens.*

Darkness and devils!

Saddle my horses! Call my train together!

Degenerate bastard, I'll not trouble thee;

Yet have I left a daughter.

*He pulls the cloak tighter, standing straighter. For a
moment, he almost believes himself powerful again. But
the weight of the words catches. Warmth seeps from his*

voice, replaced by something brittle, something close to
pleading.

Woe that too late repents!

O, sir, are you come?

Is it your will? Speak, sir! Prepare my horses!

He lifts the cloak slightly—as though expecting it to still
command authority—but it is only rags. It slips from his
grasp. He catches it, but his hands hesitate. His mouth
tightens.

Ingratitude, thou marble-hearted fiend,

More hideous when thou show'st thee in a child

Than the sea-monster!

His body turns sharply—rage surging—the cloak
whipping behind him with the motion. For a moment, it
almost resembles a king's mantle again. But the moment
is brief.

Detested kite! Thou liest!

His fingers dig into the fabric, twisting it into his
fists—as if trying to crush something in his grasp.

My train are men of choice and rarest parts,

That all particulars of duty know

And in the most exact regard support

The worships of their name.

A brittle laugh escapes him. He shakes the cloak, as
though presenting proof—but there is nothing left to
show. Nothing left to command.

O most small fault,

How ugly didst thou in Cordelia show!

Which, like an engine, wrench'd my frame of nature

From the fix'd place; drew from my heart all love

And added to the gall.

> *A sudden, violent motion—his hands leave the fabric,*
> *clawing at his own head. A surge of self-recrimination.*

O Lear, Lear, Lear!

> *He strikes his own head—once, twice—then lets the*
> *cloak fall. It pools at his feet. A discarded thing.*

Beat at this gate that let thy folly in

And thy dear judgment out!

> *A long pause. He expects movement. None. A flicker of*
> *fear. Quickly buried. He sways slightly, looking down at*
> *the fallen cloak.*

Go, go, my people.

> *But there are no people. No train. No power left to*
> *summon. He stares at the lifeless heap of fabric,*
> *then—suddenly—he drops to his knees beside it. His*
> *hands reach for it, almost without thinking.*

It may be so, my lord.

Hear, Nature, hear! Dear goddess, hear!

> *He spreads the cloak over his lap, hands gripping it*
> *tightly. For a moment, it is something living again.*
> *Something he might still command.*

Suspend thy purpose, if thou didst intend

To make this creature fruitful.

Into her womb convey sterility;

Dry up in her the organs of increase;

And from her derogate body never spring

A babe to honour her!

> *With each curse, his hands tighten. He pulls the fabric*
> *closer, as though gripping his daughters' very flesh. His*
> *breath quickens. His hands shake violently.*

If she must teem,

Create her child of spleen, that it may live

And be a thwart disnatur'd torment to her.

> *His fingers tighten—and then, suddenly, he presses the*
> *cloak against his chest. Holding it like something sacred.*
> *Holding it like a child.*

Let it stamp wrinkles in her brow of youth,

With cadent tears fret channels in her cheeks,

Turn all her mother's pains and benefits

To laughter and contempt, that she may feel

How sharper than a serpent's tooth it is

To have a thankless child!

> *The words hang in the air. His breath is unsteady. He*
> *looks around—as if suddenly realizing the walls have*
> *closed in. The cloak, now lying crumpled again, stares*
> *back at him. The storm rages inside him.*

No, no, they would not!

They durst not do't;

They would not, could not do't.

His gaze falls. A tremor.

O, reason not the need!

His hands reach for the fabric once more—but this time,
trembling. Fingers brush over it, not lifting it yet. Just
feeling its weight.

Our basest beggars

Are in the poorest thing superfluous.

Allow not nature more than nature needs,

Man's life is cheap as beast's.

Finally—his arms gather the cloak again. He presses it
against himself. His body rocks slightly.

I will have such revenges on you both

That all the world shall—I will do such things—

What they are yet, I know not; but they shall be

The terrors of the earth!

But the fire flickers out. His body curls inward, folding
over the fabric. The weight of loss presses into him.

You think I'll weep.

A long pause. His breath hitches.

No, I'll not weep.

His grip on the cloak loosens slightly.

I have full cause of weeping, but this heart

Shall break into a hundred thousand flaws

Or ere I'll weep.

His head lifts slightly. His voice—soft now. Slipping
into something close to pleading.

O, let me not be mad, not mad, sweet heaven!

Keep me in temper; I would not be mad!

But even as he clings to the cloak, his body trembles. His fingers press into the fabric—searching, pressing—but finding nothing. He is slipping.

A long silence. He stands in the wreckage of his mind, trembling. The betrayal has already happened, yet he is still in it, reliving it, unable to escape. The cloak remains wrapped around him, but now, instead of the burden of a king, it is a shroud.

SCENE V: THE FOOL'S ECHO & MADNESS CREEPING

A shift. The walls of his daughters' halls dissolve into darkness. Lear stands alone. Or perhaps not. A shape in the shadows, a voice just out of reach. The Fool? Cordelia? Or only his own thoughts turning against him? The cloak clings to his shoulders. He shudders.

LEAR

Dost thou call me fool, boy?

He listens. A pause. A ghost of a smile flickers at the edges of his mouth. The Fool would have had an answer for that. The Fool—where is he? His hand drifts to the cloak, absently, as though expecting to find him there.

No more of that; I have noted it well.

He nods to some unseen figure. Then—a pause. His fingers toy with the cloak's frayed hem. A whisper—uncertain—

Go you and tell my daughter I would speak with her.

He waits. Silence. His voice sharpens.

Go you, call hither my Fool.

Still nothing. His smile fades. The air is empty. He shivers, pulling the cloak tighter, wrapping it around himself—not in power, but in need. Like a child clutching a comfort.

A flicker of something—a memory? A laugh? He shakes his head. He does not want to hear it.

Come on, my boy.

How dost, my boy? Art cold?

His hands gather the cloak up, holding it against his chest, as if there were another body there. The Fool? A memory? Himself? His voice lowers—confessional.

I am cold myself.

The wind picks up again—or perhaps it is only in his head. The fabric ripples slightly. His brow furrows. The Fool is speaking—but Lear cannot hear. A forced laugh escapes him, sharp, brittle. His grip tightens. He cannot let go.

Thou think'st much that this contentious storm
Invades us to the skin.
So 'tis to thee;
But where the greater malady is fix'd,
The lesser is scarce felt.

A pause. His mind shifts. A spiral. The cloak twists with him as he turns. His breath quickens. His head lifts—wild-eyed.

Let the great gods,
That keep this dreadful pudder o'er our heads,
Find out their enemies now.

He throws the cloak open, spreads it wide. A throne. A courtroom. A corpse. It shifts, slipping between them, refusing to be one thing. He grips the edges, twisting the fabric, willing it to hold. Willing it to obey.

Tremble, thou wretch,
That hast within thee undivulgèd crimes,
Unwhipp'd of justice.

Hide thee, thou bloody hand;

Thou perjur'd, and thou simular man of virtue

That art incestuous.

> *His gaze pierces the folds of the fabric, as if seeing ghosts*
> *there. His voice sharpens, fevered.*

Caitiff, to pieces shake,

That under covert and convenient seeming

Hast practis'd on man's life!

> *The wind howls. The cloak flutters violently, pulling*
> *against his grip. He clutches it close again, curling*
> *around it—a man holding onto the thing that is*
> *damning him.*

Close pent-up guilts,

Rive your concealing continents, and cry

These dreadful summoners grace!

> *He staggers back, then forward. His grip tightens,*
> *loosens, tightens again. His gaze—fixed downward. The*
> *cloak is the courtroom. The cloak is the accused. The*
> *cloak is the trial.*

I will arraign them straight.

> *His head snaps up. His hand lifts—pointing at*
> *nothing. Summoning a trial from the air.*

Come, sit thou here, most learned justicer.

> *He tugs the cloak up over his shoulder, twisting it,*
> *shaping it—as if making a seat, a bench, a throne for*
> *judgment. His tone turns sharp, accusing.*

Thou, sapient sir, sit here.

To another unseen presence. His hand gestures toward a
hollow space within the fabric, where a shadow might sit.

Now, you she-foxes!

He leans forward, breath quickening. His fingers curl
into the cloak's edges, as though grasping at the very
bodies of the accused.

Arraign her first. 'Tis Goneril.

A shadow passes through him. A flicker of the past.
His head shakes violently—his grip tightens. He is
holding her there. Holding her in the fabric.

I here take my oath before
this honourable assembly, she kicked the poor King her father.

He listens. Waiting for a defense. The cloak rustles. His
eyes widen. Fury rising.

She cannot deny it.

His hands lift the fabric, shaking it, as if shaking the
truth from it. He presses it into his chest. The accusation
cannot be escaped.

And here's another, whose warp'd looks proclaim
What store her heart is made on.

A beat. A tremor passes through him. He freezes. His
breath stills.

Stop her there!
Arms, arms! Sword! Fire!
Corruption in the place!

171

The cloak shifts— does it move on its own? His hands
falter. A realization—he is holding nothing. He pulls
the cloak away suddenly, as though burned.

False justicer, why hast thou let her scape?

He reels back. The trial dissolves. The hallucination
fractures. The figures vanish. The voices fade. He stands
alone. Trembling. The cloak crumples against his
chest—lifeless again.

The little dogs and all,

Tray, Blanch, and Sweetheart, see, they bark at me.

A beat. He closes his eyes. The fabric shifts in his grip.
His fingers loosen. When he speaks, it is barely a
whisper.

O, that way madness lies; let me shun that;

No more of that.

But even as he says it, his hands tighten. He pulls the
cloak closer again, folding into it, trembling. The weight
of it drapes over him—a shroud, a memory, a thing he
cannot put
down.
The wind dies. The shadows remain.

SCENE VI: THE BROKEN KING & THE NAKED TRUTH

> *A shift. The storm has passed. Or perhaps it has only moved inward. Silence, but not peace. Lear stands, shivering. His garments—soaked, clinging to his skin. His crown—long since slipped away. The cloak—once a symbol of power, then a shroud of madness—now hangs in sodden folds around him. It is as tattered as he is. It weighs on him.*
>
> *He peers into the darkness. And then—movement. A figure. Ragged. Wild. "Poor Tom." Or something Lear believes him to be.*

LEAR

Hast thou given all to thy two daughters,

And art thou come to this?

> *He steps closer, his breath visible in the cold. His hands grip the cloak, pulling it tighter, as if for warmth—or as if in disbelief. He peers at the man before him.*
>
> *But—is it Poor Tom? Or is it his own reflection? He shudders.*

What, have his daughters brought him to this pass?

Couldst thou save nothing? Didst thou give 'em all?

> *He reaches forward—but stops. His fingers hover in the empty space between them, trembling. He sways slightly. A whisper of wind. The weight of it all presses down on him. The cloak sags from his shoulders.*

Now all the plagues that in the pendulous air

Hang fated o'er men's faults light on thy daughters!

> *A beat. His grip on the cloak tightens. A sharper*
> *breath—pleading, accusing, breaking.*

Death, traitor!

Nothing could have subdu'd nature

To such a lowness but his unkind daughters.

> *His hands press against the fabric at his chest, gripping*
> *it like a wound. The cloak is all he has left. The last*
> *thing between himself and the truth.*

Is it the fashion that discarded fathers

Should have thus little mercy on their flesh?

> *A sudden laugh—a raw, brittle sound. Then—he*
> *throws the cloak open, spreading it wide, displaying the*
> *emptiness left behind. The ruin of him.*

Judicious punishment!

'Twas this flesh begot those pelican daughters!

> *The words hang in the air. His hands shake. His breath*
> *is ragged. He looks down—at the cloak draped over*
> *him, at his body beneath it. He steps back, staring at his*
> *own hands, his own skin, as if trying to understand it.*
> *Then—an epiphany. Terrible in its clarity. His voice*
> *drops. Barely above a whisper.*

What hast thou been?

> *He waits. There is no answer. Or perhaps—he is the*
> *answer. His gaze hardens.*

Thou wert better in thy grave

Than to answer

With thy uncover'd body

This extremity of the skies.

A sharp breath. His body shudders. A revelation is
upon him. His fingers trace the edges of the
cloak—hesitant.
And then—suddenly—he rips it from his shoulders.
The fabric falls to the ground.
Is man no more than this?
He stares at the fallen cloak. His shoulders rise and fall.
His breath is unsteady.
Then—he steps over it.
He steps away from it.
As if freeing himself.

Consider him well.

Thou ow'st the worm no silk,

The beast no hide,

The sheep no wool,

The cat no perfume.

His breath quickens. His voice rises.

Ha!

Here's three on's are sophisticated!

He lets out a strangled laugh. A bitter, unraveling
sound. Then—his voice trembles. Something raw, honest,
breaking through.
His fingers tremble at his collar. A realization. An
undoing.

Thou art the thing itself!

And then—in a fevered motion—

Off, off, you lendings!

Come, unbutton here!

*He tears at his clothing, stripping away the last
remnants of royalty, of dignity, of self. The cloak is gone.
The weight is lifted.*

*His body shakes from the cold. But—he does not cover
himself.*

For a moment, he just stands there.

Exposed.

Vulnerable.

Reduced to nothing but flesh and breath.

He breathes.

A long silence. The storm is gone. The king is gone.

Only a man remains.

SCENE VII: CORDELIA & THE FRAGILE HOPE

A shift. Time fractures again. The cold, naked truth of Lear's madness fades into something softer—warmer, even. The edges of memory blur.

The cloak is gone.

He is no longer in the wilderness. He is somewhere safe. Or is he?)

He blinks. Breath slow, unsteady. Shifting, disoriented.

Before him—Cordelia. Or the idea of her. His breath catches.

His fingers twitch, reaching for something—someone—just beyond his grasp.

LEAR

You do me wrong to take me out o' th' grave.

A flicker of recognition—or confusion. He stares at her, eyes wide, blinking against the light.

Thou art a soul in bliss, but I am bound
Upon a wheel of fire, that mine own tears
Do scald like molten lead.

He lifts a trembling hand, as if to touch her, afraid she might vanish. His fingers hesitate, hover in the air.

You are a spirit, I know.
When did you die?

He waits for an answer, but none comes. His frown deepens. He searches her face, trying to place himself, trying to place her.

Where have I been?

Where am I?

> *A moment. His voice wavers—fear, grief, disbelief. He glances around, as if seeing the world for the first time.*

Fair daylight?

> *He squints into the light. His fingers twitch, flexing. He looks down at his hands, his body, as though unfamiliar with them.*

I am mightily abus'd.

I should e'en die with pity,

To see another thus.

I know not what to say.

> *He presses his hands together, testing their weight, their reality. He turns them over, as if they do not belong to him.*

I will not swear these are my hands.

Let's see.

> *He grips his own fingers, pressing them into his palm, as if searching for sensation, for proof.*

I feel this pin prick.

> *He flinches. A beat. Then, a breath—a whisper. A moment of fragile recognition.*

Would I were assur'd

Of my condition!

> *And then—he looks at her again. Really looks. A fragile hope trembles in his voice.*

Pray, do not mock me.

> *A beat. The words are soft, almost childlike.*

I am a very foolish, fond old man,

Fourscore and upward, not an hour more nor less;

And, to deal plainly,

I fear I am not in my perfect mind.

> *His voice catches. His gaze drifts to something unseen,*
> *his mind still unraveling, still trying to stitch itself*
> *together.*

Methinks I should know you, and know this man.

> *He gestures vaguely—perhaps at a figure that isn't really*
> *there. The past and present war within him.*

Yet I am doubtful, for I am mainly ignorant

What place this is; and all the skill I have

Remembers not these garments; nor I know not

Where I did lodge last night.

> *A plea now—desperate, fragile. He turns to her, as if*
> *begging for reassurance.*

Do not laugh at me.

> *A breath. A silence. The world feels still, suspended in a*
> *delicate balance.*

For, as I am a man,

I think this lady

To be my child Cordelia.

> *He waits. She does not vanish. His fingers twitch again.*
> *He takes a breath. His voice drops to a whisper—*

Be your tears wet?

> *A pause. A fragile smile.*

Yes, faith.

Something shifts. A deep, tired sigh. The old anger, the old wounds stir inside him—but they are duller now, like a blade long buried. His breath slows. His hands unclench.

I pray, weep not.

And then, softly—

If you have poison for me,
I will drink it.

He shakes his head, a bitter chuckle—half a joke, half the deepest truth. A breath. A pause. Then—

I know you do not love me.

But the memory returns—his daughters, their cruelty, their betrayal. His body tenses slightly. He looks at her again, the words slipping from his lips before he can stop them.

For your sisters
Have, as I do remember, done me wrong.

A breath.

You have some cause, they have not.

He watches her, waiting—expecting hatred, expecting punishment. Instead, something like love lingers in the air. His lips part slightly. He blinks, overwhelmed.

Am I in France?

He searches her face for confirmation. For something solid. For something real.

Do not abuse me.

A pause. A hesitation. And then—acceptance. A surrender.

You must bear with me.

His voice drops. No longer that of a king, but of a broken man.

Pray you now, forget and forgive.

A beat.

I am old and foolish.

A long silence. Perhaps the gentlest moment in the play. For the first time, Lear is neither king nor madman. He is simply a father. A man longing to be forgiven.

VIII. The Final Blow

> *Lear stands, holding something—someone. A weight in his arms. His cloak, twisted, draped, is tangled within her form. Or is it? His arms tighten around it. For a moment, it is just fabric. For a moment, it is just her. The lines blur.*

LEAR

Howl, howl, howl, howl!

> *He staggers, swaying beneath the weight. His breath shudders. His body shudders.*
> *A shift. He kneels—slow, heavy. The cloak pools around them both. He grips it tightly, pressing his face into it, as if breathing her in.*

O, you are men of stone.

Had I your tongues and eyes, I'd use them so

That heaven's vault should crack.

> *His hands shake. His fingers, woven into the fabric, tighten.*

She's gone forever!

> *He spreads out the cloak, then meticulously folds it - starting one corner, one fold, then the next corner and so on. It takes him until nearly the end of the scene to have the full swaddled bundle that is, for him, Cordelia's corpse.*

I know when one is dead, and when one lives.

He brings a trembling hand to her lips, holding it there,
waiting for warmth, for breath—

She's dead as earth.

A silence. He closes his eyes. No. No, he cannot accept
it. His voice, suddenly sharp, commanding—

Lend me a looking glass;
If that her breath will mist or stain the stone,
Why, then she lives.

He waits. Nothing. He cannot look away. And then—

This feather stirs!

Hope. Wild, impossible hope. His breath quickens—

She lives!

A desperate, broken laugh—one that barely escapes
before his body folds inward again.

If it be so,
It is a chance which does redeem all sorrows
That ever I have felt.

He folds the last corner—then stops. His fingers hover
over the unfinished bundle. A long, wavering pause. His
breath catches. He stares down, willing the thing in his
arms to be whole, to be real. But it is only cloth. Only
loss.

A plague upon you, murderers, traitors all!
I might have sav'd her—now she's gone forever!

He grips Cordelia to his chest, rocking.

Cordelia, Cordelia! Stay a little. Ha!

A beat. Then, softer—

What is't thou say'st?

A pause. A deep breath, as if listening. His voice
cracks—

Her voice was ever soft,

Gentle, and low—an excellent thing in woman.

He nods, as if this should mean something. As if this
should change something. His head turns slightly.

I kill'd the slave that was a-hanging thee.

A hollow exhale. The admission means nothing now.

Did I not, fellow?

He barely hears the response. His mind is slipping,
breaking apart like an old tree in the wind. He blinks,
looking around as if seeing ghosts.

I have seen the day, with my good biting falchion

I would have made them skip.

A strange, distant smile, lost in memory.

I am old now,

And these same crosses spoil me.

He frowns, peering at the shapes before him.

Who are you?

He squints—his vision failing, his mind failing—

Mine eyes are not o' th' best. I'll tell you straight.

A breath. A sigh. He looks again—

This is a dull sight. Are you not Kent?

He barely listens for the answer. His mind drifts again.

His voice is weak, distant—

He's a good fellow, I can tell you that.

He'll strike, and quickly too.

He nods to himself, as if this were important. And then—his voice falters, uncertain—

He's dead and rotten.

A pause. His body sways. His breath is shallow now, barely there.

I'll see that straight.

He struggles, as if trying to rise, to do something, to change something—but the weight, the exhaustion, the grief, it is all too much. A whisper—

You're welcome hither.

And then, the smallest of smiles—bitter, knowing.

Ay, so I think.

He looks down at the bundle. His body trembles. His final breath—a quiet, broken plea—

And my poor fool is hang'd!

A pause. His face contorts, something close to fury, close to unbearable sorrow—

No, no, no life!

A shake of the head—violence, denial—

Why should a dog, a horse, a rat, have life,
And thou no breath at all?

He clutches her to him, his face against her head, rocking, rocking, rocking. Each word slows the motion, his body winding down, the rhythm breaking apart. By the final "never," he barely moves at all. A whisper. A breath.

His fingers reach for his chest—his body is failing,
collapsing inward. A whisper—

Thou'lt come no more—

A breath. Unsteady. The weight of the word settles.

Never— (another breath, weaker now)

never— (the rocking slows, voice straining)

never— (his lips barely move now, breath nearly gone)

never— (his body is still, but one last whisper remains—)

never.

Pray you, undo this button.

A long pause. There is no button. It's his heart failing.
Then, a weak, distant—

Thank you, sir.

His breath slows. His eyes begin to unfocus. He barely
manages—

Do you see this?

He grips Cordelia to his chest, rocking. His hands press
into the fabric, holding, holding—then a flicker. A
hesitation. His fingers twitch, as though feeling the
emptiness beneath them. A sharp breath—does he
understand? If he does, it is too late. He clutches the
bundle tighter. He cannot let go.

Look there, look—

A breath catches. A flicker—like he is about to speak.
Then—nothing. He lies curled up with the bundle. His
body goes still. He looks like a sleeping child with a
teddy bear.

A long pause. The world does not stop.

Blackout.

GHOSTS OF THE GILDED STAGE

CHARACTER

ALBAN MATTHEWS

Not young. Theatre is in his bones.

He doesn't monologue. He remembers aloud.
He doesn't confess. He unpacks.
He doesn't ask for sympathy.

He wears:

- A sport coat that used to be tailored

- A black T-shirt that's seen a hundred callbacks

- Soft jeans

- Velvet slippers

- A winter scarf

Not styled. Just lived in.

SETTING

An empty stage.

The time is now—or close enough.

There is no fourth wall.

A ghostlight stands stage left. Lit. Bare bulb, steel cage.

A faded, gilded trunk, center stage. Closed.

A Victorian parlor chair, worn velvet upholstery and one badly repaired leg.

A small, beat-up side table beside the Victorian chair. Nothing ornate. Could've been salvaged from the theatre's props closet. Just enough surface for two or three items.

A box marked DONATIONS.

A rubbish bin.

A brass skeleton key on the little table. Not hidden. Not offered. Just there.

A rolling clothes rack is slightly up right.

Everything's been left, like someone meant to come back. No one did.

ACT I

The ghostlight hums.

The trunk waits.
The chair sits askew.
Empty. But not unoccupied.

Light rises—not a cue, but a creeping memory.

No sound. Just space.

Alban enters from somewhere practical. A hallway. A
door. An edge.

He steps in. Pauses.
Sees the ghostlight.
The key.

He walks to the table, removes a peach from his pocket
and sets it on the table, along with his sunglasses. Turns
to the chair. Removes his sportcoat, drapes it across the
back. Straightens it, out of habit.

Pulls off his scarf, drapes it over the sportcoat.

Looks around. Remembering. Picks up the key.

ALBAN
Skeleton key.

Beat.

Stone walls. Wood floor. Cold, no matter the season.
You can STILL see the hymn numbers on the wall under seven million
coats of paint.
Costume loft above the choir. Narrow ladder nailed into the wall.

Always damp. I was always sent because I feared neither heights nor ghosts.

We needed a coat.
Officer's. Double-breasted. Brass buttons. Epaulettes.
For a duel. Or an execution. Something dramatic.

The boxes were marked by hand.

"Troubled Periods."
(shrugs) Aren't they all.

"Dignified Men." "Crowd."
 I opened one marked "Not Yet Sorted."

Inside: masks peeling at the edges. Smelled like old glue.
A cravat, curled hard with starch.
Feathers. Loose.
And one velvet hanger. Nothing on it, but ribs.

A full set of actual human ribs.
Yellowed. Curved. Hung like a necktie.

No tag.
 Just a safety pin through the bone.

I brought it down.
 Stage manager was horrified.

"Put it back!!"

So I did.

We ran a farce instead.
Actors hated it.
Audience didn't care.

Later they moved the boxes.
No one said where.
But the ladder stayed nailed to the wall.

There was a door in the fly gallery.
Locked. From the inside.

One night, during a thunderstorm,
someone heard humming behind it.
Not a song.
Just humming, like someone passing time.

Stage manager turned on the ghostlight.
Next day, it was out.
So was the storm.

Found a rope backstage once.
Coiled wrong.
Every other line was neat—
That one: snagged. Frayed in the middle.

They told me not to touch it.
So I didn't.
I stepped around it.
Even when it was in the way.

At another place, I watched the paint frame move.
No wind. No one on deck.
Movement.
Half an hour before curtain.
We went up late that night.

Silence.

The Scottish Play.

Old opera house. Western circuit stop.
Bernhardt had played there. Booth. Langtry.

We ran through the full month of October.
Closed on Halloween.

No flats. Just scaffolding.

One of the witches broke mid-performance.

Started screaming at the other witches—louder than the lines.

Lady M, in full regalia, climbed up the back of the scaffold, dragged the
crazy witch down by the back of her collar, and threw her out the
backstage door.

We kept the scene going.

Few nights later, the Olio curtain—been hanging a hundred thirty-five
years—
tore straight across and dropped to the stage.

Just missed the banquet table and all the actors.

Audience screamed.

And up in the boxes—
balcony rail, stairwell landing—
you could see the ghosts.

Slipping in and out.
Cast saw them.
Crew.
Audience.

He holds the key a moment longer.

Skeleton key.
Designed to enter.

He inserts the key. Turns. The lock clicks. He opens the
lid. Silence. He looks inside—at the things memory just
let loose.

And then we call it art.

Sits. Slowly. Like memory has weight. Pulls out a
sparkly sash.

I was a quiet child.
Not shy. But careful.

Beat.

My mother said I asked too many questions with my eyes.
So she gave me books.
Told me stories.
Taught me to sew. *(beat)* She was a nurse.
Knew how to stitch people together.

(smiles) She wasn't theatrical.
But she knew what stage fright looked like
in a son who hadn't said the words yet.

My father was...

He pauses. Choosing honesty over cruelty.

A man who shook hands like he was still proving something.
He didn't yell.
He just looked at me like I was a riddle
he never meant to solve.

And when he couldn't,
he left the room.

When I was six,
I wore a towel like a cape
and demanded to be called Lady Marzipan of the Moon.

My mother laughed.

My father left the room, as usual.

He didn't hit.
He just didn't stay.

A quieter kind of bruise.

> *He stays seated. Leaning forward slightly, like speaking
> to a mirror.*

I used to play dress-up with my mother's old clothes.

Not the ones she wore.
The ones she kept in the cedar chest she never opened.

I opened it.

There was a nightgown—silky.
Not see-through. But it felt expensive.

And a robe with velvet cuffs.
Sleeves too long.

There was a lipstick.
Plum Realness.

I'd smear it on in the bathroom with the fan running.

Then scrub it off before dinner
and pretend my lips were just chapped.

My mother knew.

She didn't say.

But one day, it was gone.

Replaced with a softer shade.
One that wiped off easier.

No questions.

My mother had her last at forty-two.
Worked nights for five years straight.
 Had a hysterectomy and never called it that.

Just said,
"I'm done, love."

Beat.

My parents shared a room.
But not a life.

They slept in shifts.
No one ever handed off the baton.

Mass was our calendar.
Feast days. Lent. Stations of the Cross.

The church smelled like candles and cigar smoke.

The priests loaned me old, decommissioned cassocks.
Let me rewrite the Passion Play with musical numbers.
Didn't blink when I made Herod a drag queen.

Father Francis leaned over during our final dress rehearsal and told me,
"Old actors never die, they just go back to the chorus."

He laughed.
I didn't get it.

They never touched me or any of us.
Not that way.

It was the altar boys who got me in trouble.

First–sips of communion wine behind the sacristy.
Then, fumbling touches in the vestry.
First kiss that wasn't imagined.

He was older.
Not much.
Just enough to seem sure.

He kissed me like he'd done it before.
I kissed him like I was praying.

Beat.

I had friends. Of course I did.

Two girls—Annie and Bea.
We lived on the same street.

We made up plays on Bea's front porch.

Our greatest work: The Princess and the Time-Traveling Mailman.
I played both parts.
Naturally.

Bea did sound effects.
Annie made costumes out of old pillowcases.

We charged our parents fifty cents.

My father never came.
My mother cheered like it was Broadway. *(small, fond smile)*

Eventually, the girls moved on.
Not cruelly.
Boys. Sports. Popularity. It was time.

I stayed with the mirror.
With the towel-capes.
With the record player
and my private revivals of Funny Girl.

I didn't feel lonely.

Not then.

Because in my head,
the audience always came back.

Middle school.
A substitute teacher.
A copy of *Our Town*—highlighted by three students before me.

They read it like a comedy.
I thought it was the saddest thing I'd ever heard.

And then came Midsummer.
And the sash.

Suddenly, the parts of me that were too much—
Too soft.
Too strange.
Too still—
Were necessary.

He looks out—not at us. Just past himself.

In theatre, no one asked why I stood that way.
Why I spoke with my hands.
Why I knew every lyric to Carousel, but couldn't catch a ball.

They just asked,
"Can you be off-book by Tuesday?"

I didn't come out.
I unfolded, I guess.

No drama.
No announcement.

Just one day—
a boy in the cast held my hand in the wings,
and I didn't pull away.

> *He looks down at his hands. Older. But steady.*

We kissed behind the costume rack.
Next to a broken fog machine.

It smelled like sweat
and fabric paint.

It was perfect.

> *Beat.*

No one said anything.
No one had to.

> *He exhales. Long. Quiet. Peaceful.*

And somehow,
it still feels like the safest room I've ever been in.

He reaches into the trunk. Pulls out something soft. A piece of green fabric. A faded length of tulle. He folds it once, holds it in both hands, with the sash. Smiles. Small. Honest.

AH!

My first costume piece that wasn't made from something I already owned.

I stood there—just stood—and the lighting cue hit, and someone in the front row gasped.

I wasn't cast.
I was folded in.

He lifts the fabric again. Buries his face in it, breathes it in.

And they saw me. Not the glitter. Not the part. Me.

And the way the light bounced off my little face.

Afterward, someone said,
"You looked like a star."

I believed them.

Beat.

My mother wasn't theatrical.
But she liked the sound of applause.

She said theatre made me easier to live with.

A year later, they gave me Puck. I leapt from a rolling ladder and called it flight.

(softens) I did the speech. The one they all know.

"If we shadows have offended,
Think but this, and all is mended..."

> *He lets it trail off—not forgotten. Just unnecessary.*

Then came *The Fantasticks.*
I played Matt.

My first lead.
My first stage kiss that wasn't ironic or blocked for laughs.

I sang "Soon It's Gonna Rain."

They told me I didn't have to be perfect.
I just had to mean it.

And God help me—I did.

> *He picks up the sash again. Folds it. Tags it carefully.*
> *No sadness.*

> *He hangs the sash. Gently. Lets it settle. Stays there a*
> *moment longer before turning away.*

ACT II

He reaches into the trunk. Pulls out a corset. Velvet.
Structured. Worn, but intact. He runs a hand down the
front, finds the zipper.

Cheat corset.
Front zip. No laces. No hooks.
Built for speed, not period.

But it did the job.
Cinched the waist.
Lifted what needed lifting.
You could still breathe—barely.

He steps into it. Zips it up with a single pull. The effect
is instant—not drag, not costume. Realignment. Muscle
memory.

She wore the robe over it during warmups.
Wasn't meant to be seen.

He takes a few careful steps. He turns, modest.
Familiar. Not performing—just remembering.

She opened the show from the top of a staircase.
Didn't descend.
Just stood there.
Smoking.
Like the plot owed her something.

Tech called her the ghost of musicals past.
Audience called her brave.
Some of them whispered it.

One of them sent flowers.
Gardenias.

I kept the card for a while.

Silence. He exhales. Slowly. And the shape of her stays.

She was only ever in that one show.

The Widow's Cabaret.
Original book.
Six-piece band.

We had one staircase.
Three mirrors.
A fog machine that couldn't be trusted.

Sometimes it filled the house. The night it hit the dressing rooms, the bass player finally quit.

There was a quick change in Act One.
Two dressers, a bucket of ice, and a prayer.
Never missed the cue, though. Not once.

Her second song was a tango.
She didn't dance it,
She issued commands.

We rehearsed in an old Legion Hall.
Two fluorescent lights. One working toilet.
Director screamed when a rat scampered across the floor.

The Widow said, "It's good luck. That's how we know it's alive in here."

She had a lover.
Julian.
Pretty boy. Bad with lines.

I kissed him under a red gel in every town we played.
We didn't talk much after curtain.

But once, in Regina, he held my hand when the lights blacked out early.
Neither of us said a word.

She had a monologue before the finale.
Three minutes.
No music.

Just a chair, a drink, and the ghost of her first husband.
She never blinked.
So I didn't.

> *He sits carefully. The corset shifts with him. He doesn't*
> *adjust it. He breathes against it.*

I tried to wear it again, after.
Alone.
Didn't work.

> *Silence.*

This is the same chair we used in her final scene.

That was the last show I did in heels.

I wore it the night the mayor came.
Bow on my hip. Gardenias in my hair.
Never heard what she thought of the show.

But she stayed till the end.

> *He walks back to the chair. Sits slowly, legs apart.*
> *Breath shallow. No need for drama.*

All right.

> *He unzips the corset in one motion. It sighs open.*

I'm too old to put up with that noise.

He stands again. Picks up the corset. Doesn't cradle it. Doesn't mourn it. Just holds it like a thing that's done its job. He walks to the rack. Hangs it on a padded hanger. The zipper catches. He fixes it. He pulls a tag. Ties it. Writes something short. Just enough. The rack wobbles a little as he lets go. Then he turns back to the trunk.

She never liked to be put away. But there's only so long a character gets to haunt a room.

He unties a ribbon. A stack of letters loosens in his hands. He holds them.

My agent sent these.
Said she was "tying up loose ends."

It was The Widow's Cabaret.
Original show. Original score.
We toured it.
Wasn't for everyone.

He reads snippets from the letters—flat. Surgical.

"Too introspective."
"Have you considered a clearer protagonist?"
"There's something here—we're just not sure what."
"We're looking for stories with more hope."

He folds the ribbon back over the top. Ties it. Pulls an empty shoe bag out of the trunk, puts the letters in it. Hangs the packet on the rack, tags it.

Then—quietly, not bitter.

But some of them—
knew exactly where and how to cut,

so it would hurt the most.

He turns. One letter remains. He picks it up. Looks at it. Folds it. Slips it into the pocket of his sportcoat. A beat. Softer—like something escaping by accident.

I've got about six months.
Give or take.

Got the news in a mauve room with a laminate desk and a fake plant trying its best.
The doctor was kind.
The lighting was not.

Beat.

They said I could still perform.
"Within reason."

He pulls from the trunk a heavy old scrapbook bursting at the seams with clippings. Flips it open.

Ah. The juvenilia.

Before "range."
Before nuance.

Regional theatre, touring Shakespeare, a few musicals I had no business being in—
and yet, the critics came.

And they wrote.
They wrote like they were auditioning for America's Next Top Theater Snob.

He clears his throat. Reads.

"Mr. Matthews throws himself into the role of Lysander with the abandon of a young man who's never been told no."

"An enthusiasm that borders on criminal."

"He crosses the stage like a catwalk model doing Chekhov."

He smirks, crosses to the chair and sits, savoring the memories.

That one came from the Toledo Independent Review.
The critic signed it "Delphinia."
She was not subtle.

He flips the page.

"A performance of such intensity and commitment that one wonders if Mr. Matthews has recently escaped from somewhere."

"His Benedick is foppish, furious, and—frankly—feral. I enjoyed it more than I should have."

That was from the Santa Fe Beacon. Turned out to be a retired drama teacher with a schapps addiction.

"Matthews' Romeo has the posture of someone who's eaten too much for breakfast."

"Juliet didn't deserve him. The audience didn't either."

That one was laminated.
By me.

"He enters like a storm in eyeliner and exits like a curse."

I was wearing a sheer blouse and three rosaries.
Mercutio had never looked so Papist.

He flips faster now, enjoying it.

"Mr. Matthews simmers with the sort of sex appeal that has no business in family theatre."

"He acts like he's been dared to seduce the whole front row. And wins."

Beat. Laughs.

That one was from the Chicago Tribune.
Sunday matinee.
They ran the review next to an ad for carpet cleaning and a recipe for persimmon aspic.

> *He turns another page. This section's glued more carefully. The scissors were steadier. He was still trying to make it look professional. The tone changes slightly.*

And then came the contradictions.

I played Richard Three in a converted funeral home in Denver.
We used real crutches.
The hump was made from upholstery foam and hot glue.

Reads.

"Matthews' Richard is slick, sharp, and unhinged. He slinks across the stage like a cocktail party sociopath."

Great, right?

Same show. Different city.

"This Richard snarls and purrs, but offers no weight. Like watching a cobra read cue cards."

Beat.

And then, my favorite—

"Mr. Matthews' villainy is so deliciously over-the-top, I expected him to bite someone. He didn't. I was disappointed."

She underlined it three times.
My mother.

He flips.

"His Puck is not so much mischievous as mildly threatening. Like a mime with a grudge."

I got that on opening night.
Second night, same paper.

"Matthews brings such gravity to Puck that the play begins to feel like Hamlet with glitter."

Beat.

I asked the reviewer at curtain call what changed.

He said, "I was sober tonight."

He sighs. Not bitter. Just honest.

This is where I started learning:
You can't follow the praise.
It's a house of mirrors.
Some see a prince.
Some see a ghost.
Some are too busy flirting with their own regret to see anything at all.

He turns another page. Pauses. Reads with a smirk.

"Mr. Matthews plays John Proctor like he's trying to seduce the court."

"Powerful, yes. But confusing."

She signed it "Miss Agatha Penelope Crane."
Then mailed me her hotel key.
Room 407.
She'd circled it in lipstick.

Silly twat.

> *Beat. He chuckles, then sighs. The scrapbook closes a little.*

That's when I started to wonder—

What if they weren't wrong?

What if I really was seducing them?
What if I mastered admiration before I ever touched belief?

> *He taps the cover of the book.*

And then—
The cult years.

> *Beat.*

Strasberg.
Adler.
Morris.

The Holy Trinity of Emotional Damage.

I chased them like salvation.
Each one promising to break me open the right way.

He slides into a Strasberg impression—low, trembling, intimate.

STRASBERG:
"You're carrying something in your stomach. What is it? Is it shame? Is it your father? Let it leak into the monologue."

It was gas.
I was 24 and on a cabbage-heavy diet.

Beat.

Strasberg demanded your childhood.
Adler demanded your dreams.
Morris just wanted a sea sponge.

They all told me I was close.
"On the edge of something."
Nobody ever told me what.

Six months crying into a rehearsal chair like I was paying rent on the trauma.
Did a full showcase playing a man who'd lost his dog.

Beat.

I've always been a cat person.

> *He pauses. Posture shifts—shoulders square, nose up. Pretentious. Adler.*

ADLER:
"Darling, Hamlet doesn't need your diary. He needs your imagination. Picture your soul with better lighting."

> *He leans back now—lazy, broken, bitter. Morris.*

MORRIS:
"Let the emotion find you. Don't pursue it. Let it happen. Be the barnacle."

I didn't feel like a barnacle.
I felt like a fraud.

Beat.

I tried to feel something. Instead, I learned to fake it better.

And then I went the other way.
Outside-in.
Let the wardrobe make the man.
Don't choose—let the boots decide.

I built entire characters around wigs.

One director called it "shallow."
Another called it "fascinating."
Neither asked me to come back.

He folds his hands, gently.

Eventually, I stopped choosing technique.
Let the play tell me what it needed.

He exhales. Low chuckle.

The truth is...
You only find your process after you've survived everyone else's.

Beat.

Meisner got it right.

After all the sobbing in chairs,
after Strasberg dug through my childhood like a dog under a fence,
after Adler told me to imagine grief as a chandelier,
after Eric Morris made me crawl on the floor and hiss at my own
reflection—

Meisner said, "Do something."

Not feel.
Not remember.
Just—act.

> *He shifts. More grounded now. Less theatrical. More actor-in-rehearsal.*

Independent activity.

Clean the table.
Polish a shoe.
Peel an orange.
Let the line hit you mid-fold, mid-scrub, mid-whittle.

It saves you.
Because suddenly it's not about the goddamn performance.
It's about getting the stain out.

> *Beat.*

When I played Lopakhin – I was far too young, but we all were. We were our own young company that was going to redefine the art form. *(laughs)* We were pretentious idiots. BUT - that was when I finally cracked it.

I folded shirts in Act II.
Nobody told me to.
It just happened.

By week two, the director stopped me and said,
"Why are you folding laundry all the time?"

And I didn't know.
I just knew I loved the way it felt.

So I looked at him and said—off the cuff— "Not laundry. I'm unpacking my old life. Folding it into the furniture of my new one."

Beat. Shrugs.

Director blinked once, said,
 "Keep it."

Beat.

The words affect the action.
The action carries the weight.
Not your face.
Not your pain.
The cloth in your hand.
The floor beneath you.

Do something.

And that's when Hamlet came calling.

Twenty-seven.
Lean. Hollow-eyed.
The kind of age where you still believe grief can be memorized.

We mounted it in Chicago.
Not Steppenwolf—but close enough to smell the ambition and greasepaint.
Exposed brick, ten borrowed lights, and a skull that smelled like mildew from 1937.

I lived on apples and black coffee.
I flirted with Nietzsche.
It worked on exactly one stage manager.
I wore a turtleneck like the bastard child of bourbon and Chekov.

He lets that hang. Beat. A dry smile.

God, I thought I was dangerous.

I thought I'd taken action-based performance to its purest form
where thinking *felt* like movement.
I'd been watching way too much French art film.

I broke it open one vowel at a time.
Every pause was intentional.
Every moment: scored, timed, framed.

> *He removes the laminated clipping from its sleeve. The
> paper doesn't bend. It's been folded, unfolded,
> remembered.*

The Tribune came second Friday.
Third row, center aisle.
He wore a trench coat.

Blaine—Osric, over-powdered and over-invested—came backstage
mid-fight call, breathless, said, "He's here."

Grinning like he'd just discovered ice cream.

Silly old cow.

> *Beat. He reads. Not mocking. Not mournful. Just
> plain.*

"Mr. Matthews brings clarity and control to the role of Hamlet."

"Each soliloquy is sculpted. Each movement measured."

"This is a Hamlet that understands the text, but fears the emotion
beneath it."

"One admires the precision. One longs for the pain."

> *He lowers the review. Just breathes.*

That was it.

Not cruel.
Not kind.
Just surgical.

And it wrecked me.

Because I knew—
He was right.

Beat.

I didn't unravel. I presented.
Didn't descend. Just... delivered.

I didn't grieve.
I gave a TED talk.

*He folds the clipping back into thirds. Neat. Like it
always has been. Like it always will be.*

That didn't drive me out of the land of the free and the home of the
brave. That came later.

But this was the first time I really got it.

Perfection isn't the point.
Presence is.

And I wasn't there.

*Begins to close the book, but one last clipping catches his
eye.*

"Alban Matthews as Lucentio moved with all the sensual grace of a
ferret in a wet Speedo."

Laughing, he crosses to the table and puts the scrapbook under his sunglasses and peach. He goes to the trunk. Pulls out a heavy, crimson, water-stained cloak with royal trim. He shrugs it on—loose. The sleeves hang long. The collar's off-center. He doesn't fix it.

Richard Two.
The speech.
The mirror.
The fall.

You only get one of those. If you're lucky.

He stands still a moment. Then—almost unconscious—

"Ay, no; no, ay; for I must nothing be…"

He looks to the audience. Crooked smile.

That's how it starts.
Wrecked half the cast.
No one knew when to breathe.

"Therefore no 'no,' for I resign to thee…"

He turns over the crown. In words. Not gesture. It's all language. Power reduced to poetry.

"Now mark me how I will undo myself…"

I asked to cut that line.
Director said, "Absolutely not."
Called it the spine of the scene.

It felt like a warning.

"I give this heavy weight from off my head…"

He mimes the gesture. Slowly.

"…And this unwieldy sceptre from my hand…"

We used a walking stick.
Props said it had gravitas.
Truth was—they didn't want to dig deeper in storage.

Called it an artistic choice.
Said the wear made it noble.

It was splintered.
Like most of us.

Back then, I had to pretend the weight hurt.

He looks down. As if into a mirror.

"With mine own tears I wash away my balm,
 With mine own hands I give away my crown…"

They clapped.
For the speech, obviously.
Not for the actor.

"All pomp and majesty I do forswear…"

Too hot.
Too bright.
Almost passed out in Act Three.
No one noticed.
I kept going.

"…And my large kingdom for a little grave…"

Beat.

"For God's sake, let us sit upon the ground
and tell sad stories of the death of kings..."

During my last infusion, the guy in the next chair said, "I wish they had
those rainbow popsicles we got as kids."
He couldn't remember what they were called.
I knew exactly what he meant.
I can't remember the name either.
But my mouth starts watering when I think of them.

"For within the hollow crown..."

*He steps forward. The robe now only fabric, no longer
armor.*

There was a boy in the cast—
Fresh out of drama school.
Full of Grotowski and coconut oil.

He told me to deliver the whole speech seated.
Said it grounded the fall.

I told him to ground himself where the spotlight don't shine.

"Keeps Death his court..."

He stops. Stillness. A breath.

"For God's sake..."
(soft, almost apologetic) "...let us sit upon the ground
and tell sad stories of the death of kings."

He smiles—bittersweet. Removes the robe. Tags it.

I sat too early once.
Missed the cue.
Bolingbroke froze.

We called it the royal pause.

One dry laugh. It echoes once, then dies. Stops, speaks directly to the audience.

I wonder what you were promised tonight.

He reaches into the trunk. Slower now. His hand pauses, then pulls out a small card—creased, smudged, the kind they hand out at table reads. He reads it and quickly flings it onto the chair.

FUCK me. How the FUCK did that get in there?!

Beat.

I sure as fuck didn't save it.

Beat.

Every actor has one show that felt like salvation.
That one project that made you believe it all meant something.

This was mine.

New play. Brilliant script.
"Experimental realism," they called it.
Which meant no one knew what the hell they were doing,
but God, we believed in it.

Small cast.
Bare stage.
All pain, no set.

Beat.

Director said he saw me.
"Alban, this part lives in your marrow."
I said, "Good. That's where the bruises are."

He half-smiles, bitter. Then drops it.

We rehearsed for seven weeks.
He rewrote scenes during blocking improvs.
Called it collaboration.

The role was mine.
I had the contract. The fittings. The monologue in my sleep.

Understudy rehearsal.

He used my breath. My rhythm. Like he'd written it.

Then Equity called.
Said the producers were buying out my contract.
Two weeks' severance.
"Nothing personal."

Beat.

I called that bitch.
No answer.
Left a message with the company manager.
Never got a call back.

Dropped by the theatre the next day—
Nobody made eye contact.
Nobody said a word.

Long silence.

Theatre's supposed to be family.
 Especially opening week.

Especially when it's falling apart and you're holding each other with spirit gum and spike tape.

Long pause. He doesn't move.

Seven weeks.
My name.
Just gone.

Beat. Rage begins to push through the calm.

After the show, the director told me,
"You're too internal.
You disappear."

He unfolds the scarf. Rough. Like it's a wound.

I disappeared.

No.

I was erased.

Beat.

Later, I learned it was agreed—I was 'too light in the loafers.'

That's what they called it then.
Not "queer." Not "gay."
Just... light.
Like it was a wardrobe note.
Like I could butch it up for the second act.

(vehemently) I played Stanley.
Stanley! John Proctor. Mark Antony.
Not once a Tom.

Beat. Smaller now.

We had wives. In scripts and in life.
My first "wife" was a lighting designer named Julia.
She needed a green card. Bingo!

The crew called her my beard.
She called me family.

We fled to Canada.
Said it was for work.
But really, we were chasing acceptance.

She married a woman there.
I married a man. Quietly.
In a room that smelled like lemon oil.

Back to the scarf. Quiet now.

And still—after all that—he said I "disappeared."

I was right there.

*He picks up the card like it might burn him. Flings it in
the rubbish bin.*

Act III

Back to the trunk. He pulls out a dusty top hat.
Crushed. Misshapen. Stares at it like it owes him back
pay.

Scrooge.
Annual production.
Twenty years.

Same director.
Same snow machine.
Same fake roast goose.

This one always smelled like mothballs and cheap gin.

I played him with a limp by year ten.
By year fifteen, I didn't have to fake the limp.

He puts the hat on. Just for a second. Removes it. Puts it
on top of the rack.

Kids came and went.
Taller the next season, replaced the season after that with a new crop of
urchins.

Paper chains.
Plastic snow.
Fog that coughed like a heavy smoker.

And always—always—someone in the front row
crying at the second ghost.

Some ghosts become part of the set.

He tags the hat, returns to the trunk. Slower. Pulls out
a soft brown coat. Looks heavier now.

Willy.

Poor bastard.

> *He doesn't put the coat on. He holds it like an old friend*
> *he's stopped calling.*

I played him too early the first time. Too late the last. Somewhere in the middle, I forgot how to save him.

He's not tragic because he dreams.
He's tragic because he remembers.

> *Beat.*

One night, I forgot the line about the fridge.
Stood there. Blank.

I said, "It hums, sometimes."

You forget what silence feels like in that house.
What grief sounds like when it's still married.

> *He folds the coat over his arm. Looks at it. He walks it*
> *to the rack. Hangs it. Tags it. Doesn't look back.*

They don't need me in the office anymore.

> *Beat.*

They never did.

> *He reaches into the trunk. Pulls out a shapeless*
> *cardigan. Worn, pilled, comforting.*

Grandpa in You Can't Take It With You.

Eight weeks.
One fitting.

> *He slides into the cardigan. It doesn't transform him. It reveals him.*

After curtain, a kid came up and said,
"You looked like my real grandpa."

I called that connection. For men without children, there's that.

> *He turns to the trunk. Hesitates. Then pulls out the crown—tarnished, dented, magnificent.*

I remember when I'd have given my arm to play Lear.
 Now, it's too easy.

(quiet) One for the joy.
 One for the grief.

I wore them both.

And I don't know which one fit better.

> *Beat.*

They said Lear meant you'd arrived.

No one tells you what it means when you're done.

> *He sets the crown on his head. The cardigan stays on.*

> *He steps center. The light sharpens, colder now.*

(as Lear):"Blow, winds, and crack your cheeks…"

> *Then—without changing posture—*

(as Grandpa): You forgot your boots.

(as Lear): "Rage! Blow!"

(as Grandpa): Don't yell, I'm right here.

Beat.

(as Lear): "I am a man more sinned against than sinning…"

(as Grandpa): I told them not to put onions in the meatloaf.
No one listens to Grandpa.

He shifts—ever so slightly. Posture. Breath. It's not impression. It's memory.

(as Lear): "Do you see this?"
"Look there. Look there."

(as Grandpa): I see you.
Of course I do.
You looked like you needed it.

He's both now. Lear's fire in his eyes. Grandpa's ache in his shoulders.

(as Lear): "No breath at all?"

(as Grandpa): Only enough to say goodbye.

Beat.

Light tight around him. Shadows start to grow.

(as Lear): "Do you see this?"

"Look there, look there…"

(as Grandpa): You said you knew them by sound alone.

(as Lear): "Let me wipe it first. It reeks of mortality."

229

(as Grandpa): You don't need to carry all of them.
Just the ones you can still name.

(as Lear): "Is this the promised end?"

(as Grandpa): No.
Just the lights coming down.

He lowers the crown.

Beat.

Nobody could take that from me.

Silence.

Some kings fall.
Some grandfathers shine.

I did both.
Six nights a week.

And never once did it feel like a lie.

*He walks to the chair. Sets the crown on the seat, folds
the cardigan on top of it.*

Some exits don't need applause.
Just grace. But, hey. I'm still here, right? That's something.

*He starts throwing broken old stuff away and pitching some in the donation bin. A
slow vamp begins. Alban starts humming along. Soft. Reflective. Like Alban's
singing from memory, not performance. The tune flickers between lullaby and lament.*

Old tights and pratfalls,
I've worn them all, and my dear—
I'm still here.
Stitches and sweat stains,

Quick changes, quiet with fear—
Still here.
There's thread in my coat
From a show no one saw—
But I remember.
So I'm here.

Shared scripts and silence,
Rooms with one bulb and one chair—
I'm still here.
Tech weeks and ten lines,
Curtains that never quite clear—
But I'm here.
I've cued the storm, I've played the wind,
Missed the mark,
Still leaned in—
And I'm here.

Flops with no endings,
Fans with no names on their mail—
I'm still here.
Notes full of questions,
"Is there a story to tell?"—
Well, I'm here.
You don't need a hit
To be part of the song—
You just need breath.
And I'm here.

Slower, nearly spoken.

Hope is for young ones—
Me, I'll take silence and tea—
And I'm here.
Yes, my dear.

Still here.

A quiet breath. He turns back to the ghostlight.

Everything I ever was is in this room.

He crosses to the trunk. Closes it. Slow. Final.

I always thought I'd go out with a blackout.
Or a standing ovation.

He laughs, just once, crosses to the coat rack. Begins pulling tags, reading them. One by one. Quietly.

Lot 14. Crimson cloak.
Used in two productions.
And one regrettable wedding reception.

Lot 29. Brown wool coat.
Mildew smell.
Buyer note: "Used in cosplay."

Lot 46. Single velvet glove.
No match found.
Like most of us.

They asked for a catalogue.

As if a life in the theatre were something you could bullet-point.

I used to think theatre kept things alive, but really, it teaches you how to say goodbye.

Beat.

I used to fear dementia, after seeing what it did to my mother.

Remembering is worse, I think.

He breathes. Not dramatic. Just tired. He picks up the bruised peach from the table.

The man downstairs gave me this. Said I looked like I needed it.

He sets it on the trunk. It wobbles. He steadies it.

It'll rot in a day. But he meant well.

Hope is a young man's monologue.
At my age, we settle for clarity.

He pulls one final tag from his pocket. Doesn't write on it. Just holds it for a beat, then tucks it into the trunk. Closes the lid.

They'll figure it out.

He walks back to the ghostlight.
Stands beside it. Just like in the beginning.

Hospice choir rehearsal is every day before lunch. Apparently, they need tenors. I said I could still fake a baritone if the lighting's right.

Beat.

(with resigned optimism) Old actors never die. They just go back to the chorus.

Lights fade. The ghostlight stays on.

End of Play.

EVEN UNTO DEATH

CHARACTERS

ISABELLE ROMÉE

Mother of Jeannette. Humble housewife, later a comfortable widow, keeper of the hearth. Carries grief like muscle: quiet, precise, unrelenting. She does not mourn aloud. She remembers in bread, in thread, in the sharpness of her hands. By play's end, she becomes witness, flame, and voice.

MARGOT

A Servant. Young, quiet, ever listening. A survivor of unspeakable things, she finds her voice in Isabelle's silence and becomes the keeper of memory.

JACQUES D'ARC

Isabelle's husband. Jeannette's father. Still, hard, unmovable. He carries shame beneath discipline. Does not understand what was taken until it is far too late.

PIERRE D'ARC

Jeannette's older brother. The firebrand. He ran toward the smoke. He carries rage and guilt in equal measure. Believes violence should have saved her. Cannot forgive himself that it didn't.

JEAN D'ARC

Jeannette's eldest brother. Quieter than Pierre. Still water that runs deep. Haunted.

AGNES

A woman of the village, Domrémy. Herbess, gossip, friend. Devout and devoted.

SETTING

The kitchen of a family farm. Stone, timber, one high window. A
generous, wooden table is center. A huge hearth with cooking surfaces
on both sides. A single taper glows on the shelf right of the hearth,
beside a worn icon of the Virgin.

ACT I

SCENE 1

Tuesday, May 31, 1431, Domrémy France.

Dawn. The coals have gone cold. ISABELLE kneads bread—sleeves rolled, arms thick with work and years. MARGOT stirs a pot near the hearth, slow and careful. JACQUES is a shadow in the corner, unmoving—a man outlived by his own silence.

MARGOT
(tentative) Do you want it smoother?

ISABELLE
No.
I like surprises in my teeth—reminds me I still have them.

MARGOT
(soft) Sorry.

ISABELLE
If you're going to ruin it, ruin it like you meant to.
Stir like it's keeping secrets.

MARGOT
What kind of secrets?

ISABELLE
Ghosts?

Beat.

You ever gut a fish and feel like it remembered?

MARGOT
I always thought that was the garlic.

ISABELLE chuckles—low, real. The dough slaps, slow and sticky. MARGOT wipes her hands, folds the cloth, and moves to her place by the hearth, threading her needle. She pricks her finger. Sucks it quietly.

MARGOT
Should I fetch kindling too?

ISABELLE
No.
Water.

MARGOT
It's leaking worse.

ISABELLE
(calling, without volume) Jacques.

JACQUES stirs. Crosses to the pail. He squats, fumbling wax and twine. The twine snaps. He curses under his breath.

JACQUES
That bucket's old.
Like the rest of us.

He slams the bucket down. MARGOT jumps. ISABELLE does not flinch.

JACQUES
She fixed it last time.
The pail.
The stool.
My boots.
(beat) She fixed what I broke.
Even the things I never saw.

ISABELLE
(to MARGOT) You'll need to start that seam over.

MARGOT
I didn't mean to—

ISABELLE
Meaning matters.

MARGOT
Should I... stir the pot?

ISABELLE
(shrugs) Can't hurt.

MARGOT
I'll fetch more wood.

> *She lifts the bucket and exits. The door creaks.*

JACQUES
Use the goat pail!

> *ISABELLE turns.*

ISABELLE
You'll ruin it.

JACQUES
It's clean.

ISABELLE
It's goat.

MARGOT
(offstage) I can pour slow. Keep the dregs back.

ISABELLE
(not unkind) If it smells like goat, I'll make you drink it and say thank you.

Jacques laughs—a small, fractured sound.

JACQUES
You shouldn't bake today.

ISABELLE
Bread doesn't observe a mourning period.

JACQUES
This isn't a regular morning.

ISABELLE
It hasn't been a regular morning since they crowned that coward.

She kneels by the hearth. Strikes flint. A flame catches, audibly.

JACQUES
Smoke east of the river.

ISABELLE
There's always smoke.

JACQUES
Burned three days, they said.

ISABELLE
Probably the oil merchant's by the Seine again.

MARGOT reenters. Paler. Her hands tremble. She clutches the bucket.

MARGOT
There was a man in the lane. From Dommartin.

ISABELLE
(*not turning*) And what did he bring? Eggs?

MARGOT
Ash.

> *Beat*

He said it was her.

> *Stillness. JACQUES crosses himself. MARGOT
> crosses herself. ISABELLE's hands slow.
> ISABELLE stands still a moment—then crosses
> herself.*

ISABELLE
(*quietly*) Then it's done.

> *She crosses to the Virgin icon.*

ISABELLE
You liked mornings.
Even when the frost curled under the door.
Even when the hens refused to lay.
(*her back to them*) Go on.
Both of you.

> *JACQUES lingers, then exits. MARGOT sets the
> bucket near the hearth.*

MARGOT
Do you want me to—

ISABELLE
Not now.

> *MARGOT follows JACQUES. The door clicks shut.
> ISABELLE kneads again. Each movement heavier.*

242

ISABELLE
Holy Mary, Mother of—
(sobs) No.
(beat)
You had one.
I had five.
(soft) But it only takes one daughter to crack the sky.
(holds the dough like a newborn.) Holy Mother,
You cradled your condemned Son —
Cradle her now.
She spoke too loud.
Wore the wrong clothes.
They crowned her with smoke.
Wrapped her in fire.
Called her damned.
But she was Yours.
She prayed to Your Son.
She called on the saints.
(beat) If she erred, it was with courage.
If she stumbled, it was toward Heaven.

The dough slaps—sodden, slow.

Pray for her, Blessed Mother.
(Her fingers tremble.) I gave her to God.
They gave her to the fire.

The fire pops. Isabelle flinches, but kneads on.

Holy Mary, mother of God,
plead with your son. Save her from the fires of Hell. *(covers the dough,
moves it to the upstage shelf.)* I told her the kitchen would be enough. *(beat)* I
lied.

*ISABELLE picks up a basket of clean laundry. Folds
it with the deliberation of a sacrament.*

SCENE 2

The next day, just past dawn.

The kitchen is grey and hollowed with the weight of unspoken things. The coals in the hearth sigh faintly. The light bleeds slowly across the packed earth floor. ISABELLE is again folding. MARGOT sets a bucket near the hearth. She looks out at the silent coop.

MARGOT
The brown hen's gone quiet again.

ISABELLE
She'll cluck when she's ready.
Or she won't.

MARGOT
(half to herself) I don't like it when they go silent.

Pause. MARGOT lifts the bucket and exits. Her footsteps fade into the cold air.

Jacques sits by the hearth, tamping his pipe. Movements slow, mechanical—avoidance disguised as ritual. A knock. We hear AGNES's voice outside, to MARGOT.

AGNES
(offstage) Rub some of this under your arms, girl. You look wretched.

Without speaking, JACQUES rises, passes through the low curtain into the sleeping area. Gone. Another knock. Isabelle wipes her hands. Crosses. Opens the door. AGNES enters, warmly.

AGNES
Morning.
Brought something green.
To remind you the world hasn't ended.

ISABELLE
(taking the herbs) Could've fooled me.

>*They kiss each other on each cheek. An everyday ritual,*
>*but deeper than usual, today.*

AGNES
Mint.
Rosemary.
A little thyme.
And enough gossip to scare the goats.

ISABELLE
(quiet) I'll take the mint.

>*AGNES places the herbs roughly on the table. The*
>*moment hangs.*

ISABELLE
(lower) What have you heard?

>*AGNES bruises a sprig of mint between her*
>*fingers—breathing in the sharp green. She says nothing.*

ISABELLE
(pressing) Please.

>*A beat. AGNES looks toward the Virgin icon. Then*
>*lowers her eyes.*

AGNES
(low) Rouen burned.

Three days.
Smoke so thick it choked the bells.

Isabelle folds a cloth tighter—each crease sharper.

ISABELLE
Tell me.

AGNES
(low) They denied her L'huile sainte.
She was not anointed.

ISABELLE crosses herself.

ISABELLE
I know she cried out for Christ.
I know she prayed.

AGNES
Three times.
Before the smoke took her.

ISABELLE
And where the hell was the Bishop?!

AGNES
(hard) He watched.
He made sure she'd be erased.

ISABELLE
As if she didn't live in my blood and claw her way into the world.
As if she had never played in the fields, carried water, or mended.
As if she didn't ride forth and crown the KING!

MARGOT
But if she called on Christ—
Wouldn't He—

ISABELLE
(cutting in) He hears.
He must hear.
The Blessed Mother hears.
Her saints and angels MUST hear!

AGNES
They say even some of the soldiers wept.
Eight hundred stood and watched.

ISABELLE
(quiet, shaking) The Bishop was wrong.
He damned a faithful girl.

AGNES
(sharper) We are the heretics.
For not dragging him from the altar.

> MARGOT stirs the coals at the hearth—mechanical,
> stunned.

MARGOT
(small) But there was one, wasn't there?

AGNES
(low, reluctant) One.
A friar.
Held up a crucifix so she could see it.
She warned him not to get too close to the flames.

ISABELLE
(breaking, gutted) And now I am to—what?
Carry on?
Bake bread?
Chop wood?
Smile at the priest in the square?!
(beat) HOW?!!

AGNES looks at her—exhausted beyond words.

AGNES
(soft, broken) Pray, Isabelle.
Pray very hard.

> *Silence—thick and absolute. ISABELLE's eyes close briefly. Then open—steady. She stares into the fire. AGNES gathers her things.*

AGNES
I will pray, Isabelle.
We all will.
Those of us who know —
what it is to bleed without dying,
to carry life, bury children,
to have no voice.

> *ISABELLE crosses to a small purse on the hearth, retrieves a coin and gives it to AGNES, who then slips out the kitchen door. JACQUES re-enters, the fire cracks. The light leaks a little wider across the stone floor. JACQUES shifts. Takes the pipe from his mouth—but not the weight from his back.*

JACQUES
She was doomed.

> *Isabelle turns—cloth still in hand. A pause.*

ISABELLE
You said you'd drown her if she disobeyed.

JACQUES
YOU didn't stop her.

ISABELLE
Oh, no, you didn't. *(almost threatening)* Say that again.

JACQUES
You know what I mean!

ISABELLE
Then have the spine to say it out loud.
With the same breath you used at her baptism.

> *Jacques steps forward—reaches for the cloth. She pulls it back. He grabs her wrist. MARGOT gasps. A beat. Isabelle twists free. Jacques's pipe clatters to the ground.*

ISABELLE
(to MARGOT) Pick that up.
Wipe it down.

> *MARGOT bends. Picks up the pipe with both hands. Wipes it with a cloth—reverent, deliberate. Jacques exits—violently. Isabelle crosses to the hearth, lifts the lid on the pot. Stirs once. MARGOT chops vegetables—turnips, leeks, onions—on a worn board. Isabelle watches her for a moment, then turns to fetch the broom and sweeps as if her life depends on it. The kitchen wakes. The sun finds its strength. Light spills across the stone floor.*

SCENE 3

The next day, afternoon.

ISABELLE plucks a chicken, on the table. Blood and feathers, on a sheet of coarse linen. Light leans in sideways through the high window. The fire glows low. A bee hums near the shutter. MARGOT is by the hearth, sewing. Pricks her finger, suddenly.

MARGOT
Damn—
(gasp) Forgive me, Madame!

ISABELLE
You broke no commandment. Nor Canon Law.
This is a day for four-letter prayers.

MARGOT keeps sewing. The bee buzzes near the window. ISABELLE swats gently—not to kill it, just to move it along. A knock. AGNES enters and the two women exchange cheek kisses. AGNES sets her bundle on the table, away from the chicken.

AGNES
(gruffly) Found these tucked behind the stillroom door.
Thought you might make better use of them than the mice.

AGNES opens her bundle—a few leftover roots, a jar of salt and some random herbs.

ISABELLE
(accepting them) Thank you.

A pause. MARGOT keeps sewing. AGNES lingers awkwardly. She's not here for the roots.

ISABELLE
(*quiet*) Sit a while.

AGNES
(*shaking her head*) Best not.

> *A heavier pause. Isabelle watches her. Sees the weight in her.*

ISABELLE
(*carefully*) You were in town yesterday.

AGNES
(*gruff*) Had to trade eggs for vinegar.

ISABELLE
You heard things.

> *AGNES doesn't answer. She fusses with her shawl.*

ISABELLE
(*sharper*) About her.

> *MARGOT freezes.*

AGNES
(*stiff*) People like to talk.
Not much of it worth hearing.

ISABELLE
Tell me.

AGNES
Old lies.

ISABELLE
Tell me the worst of it.

AGNES
(A long, long pause.) They say they forced her into a dress.
(beat) Said it was the law.

ISABELLE
(stiffening) Go on.

> *AGNES bruises a sprig of mint between her fingers,*
> *and her face hardens.*

AGNES
(low, reluctant) Told her it was heresy
to dress in men's clothes.
They threatened her with torture,
until she signed the paper
denying her angel voices.

ISABELLE
And still they burned her?!

AGNES
Her hands and feet—bound.
They violated her.
The guards—

ISABELLE
Dear Mother of God.

> *AGNES takes a long breath, letting it settle before*
> *speaking again.*

AGNES
She fought. But they wanted her to stay in that dress —
And when she didn't,
They called it a relapse.

ISABELLE
They had no right.
They wanted to SHAME HER!

AGNES
(soft) Women must obey, or be shamed.

ISABELLE
Please. Go now. Thank you. And please. Go.

> *AGNES leaves the bundle and goes out the kitchen door.*

ISABELLE
(to herself) She wanted angels.
She needed me.

> *MARGOT's needle stills. She speaks—not looking up.*

MARGOT
They said she should've stayed quiet.

ISABELLE
Who?

MARGOT
Everyone.
Monsieur.
The men in the square.
Old Béatrice.
Even the priest, before he lit his candle.

ISABELLE
(without looking up) And what are they saying now?

MARGOT
That she asked for it.

That she dressed wrong.
That she deserved the fire.

ISABELLE
And what do you think?

MARGOT
I think they're afraid she was right.

> *ISABELLE wipes her hands slowly on her apron.
> During the following dialogue, she bundles up the chicken
> and feathers in the cloth and moves it to a cold stone
> shelf. Washes her hands, dries them and then retrieves an
> earthenware jug with a cloth top secured with a leather
> tie. She opens the jug, soaks a wet rag in the vinegar,
> moves to the table and scrubs it.*

ISABELLE
Cowards.

MARGOT
She kept her promise. She protected herself.

ISABELLE
Her chastity. Yes. She cut her hair.
When she left us, she wore her brother's clothes.
She knew exactly what she was doing.

MARGOT
They forced her to wear the dress...

ISABELLE
Then they used it as their excuse.

MARGOT
To violate her?

ISABELLE
(quiet, steel) Yes.

> A long pause. MARGOT's hands go still. Her voice
> changes—no longer asking, but naming.

MARGOT
My father.
Then my uncle.
Then the man who brought barley on Thursdays.

> ISABELLE stops scrubbing. Looks at MARGOT,
> sadly.

ISABELLE
(softer) Child.

> Long silence. ISABELLE crosses to a shelf, retrieves a
> pitcher and pours water into a cup. Crosses back, gives it
> to MARGOT, her hand lingering when their fingers
> touch.

MARGOT
The priest said, "You're being punished."
The midwife poured vinegar between my legs.

ISABELLE
What did the people say? In your village.

MARGOT
That I was trouble.
Too pretty.
Too loud.
Too much, in the eyes.

ISABELLE
(after a breath) Like her.

MARGOT
And so they sent me away.

Beat.

They blame her.

ISABELLE resumes her scrubbing.

ISABELLE
It's easier to damn a girl
than the hands that lit the flame.

MARGOT
Even the women say it.
She should've stayed small.
Stayed home.

ISABELLE
(low, broken) I kept her small as long as I dared.
I hoped the kitchen would be enough.

MARGOT
What will you do?
Petition the Holy Father?

ISABELLE freezes.

ISABELLE
I'm a housewife.
A mother.
The Pope will not give me audience.
But…. Jacques could go to Father Gervais.
The priest could go to the Bishop.
The Bishop could write to Rome.

MARGOT
Could... or would?

ISABELLE
Would, if they had courage.

MARGOT
And if they don't?

ISABELLE
Then we kneel on broken stones and call it prayer.

> *A single cluck from the hens. The wind shifts. Boots on gravel. Heavy. Fast. Approaching. The door creaks open. PIERRE stands in the frame—mud-streaked, sleepless, cloaked in road dust and grief. JEAN behind him, equally worn. They stop. No one speaks. PIERRE crosses to ISABELLE. Falls to his knees. Takes her hands. JEAN crosses to JACQUES—who has entered silently. JEAN rests his forehead against his father's shoulder. JACQUES places one hand on his son's back—clumsy, but enough. MARGOT watches from the shadows—heartbroken, unmoving.*

ISABELLE
(quiet) Wash your hands.

> *JEAN and PIERRE cross to the basin. Wordless. One at a time. Like a ritual they wash and dry their hands. They return to the center of the room. Still armored in silence.*

JACQUES
(quiet) There was nothing to bring home.

ISABELLE
Thanks to you.

JACQUES
Woman, don't—

ISABELLE
Say it.

JACQUES
(sharper) She's dead.
They burned her.
And you—

PIERRE
(exploding) Don't you dare!

JACQUES
She filled her head with nonsense!

ISABELLE
(shouting) She filled her heart with God!

Beat.

Which of you ever dared believe her?

JEAN
(sharp) She believed enough for all of us.

PIERRE
We fought for her!

JEAN
You fought behind her.
And when the ground turned hot—you vanished.

PIERRE
(brutal) And you stayed back!
Coward in the shadows!

JEAN
(broken) I stayed.
I watched.
I saw her.
Through the smoke.
Through the flames.
She called once.
My name.
(beat) And then she didn't turn again.

JACQUES
Oh, you sanctimonious—

PIERRE
(to JACQUES) You called her a fool!

JACQUES
Better a fool than a corpse!

ISABELLE
Better a martyr than a coward.

Silence. The fire cracks.

MARGOT
(barely a breath) You left her?

Beat.

PIERRE
(gutted, softly) We should have torn down Rouen stone by stone.
We should have dragged the bishop
from his altar and burned HIM.

ISABELLE
Instead —

you bowed your heads.
You let them kill a girl....

> *Silence. Breathless. The fire spits—the broth hisses—the world does not stop.*

> *ISABELLE rinses and wrings out her cloth, then crosses to the table. Wipes it down one last time.*

ISABELLE
(quiet, almost to herself) We eat soon.
Say what you have to say.

> *Silence.*

PIERRE
(low, wrecked) There's nothing left to be said.

> *MARGOT stirs the pot once—tender, reverent. ISABELLE rinses the cloth. Folds it carefully. Sets it down next to the water basin. The hearth breathes low. The house holds.*

SCENE 4

Sunday, June 5, 1431

Late morning.

The kitchen table is simply laid: coarse bread, goat cheese, a bowl of boiled eggs, a crock of salt, a pitcher of goat's milk, a small jar of jam, a plate of spring onions.

MARGOT lays the cutlery—a knife and spoon at each place, and a cup. The door opens. ISABELLE enters, followed by PIERRE and JEAN. Their movements are careful. JEAN carries a cloth-wrapped parcel. JACQUES enters last, slower than the others. They remove overcoats, cloaks. ISABELLE removes her shawl. They wash their hands.

They gather at the table—not rushed, not reverent, just together. Once the others are seated, ISABELLE gives a slight nod. MARGOT sits. They cross themselves. Quietly. A pause.

JACQUES
(clearing his throat) Benedicite. Praised be God—our Lord Jesus Christ— *(he coughs; cannot finish.)*

JEAN
(gently) ...for the grace of this day... *(He lowers his head. Can't finish.)*

ISABELLE
(soft, sure) Benedicite.
Praised be God, our Lord Jesus Christ, for the grace of this day.
Bless, O Lord, these gifts that we receive from Your goodness.
Grant that we may serve You faithfully in all things.
Amen.

They echo "Amen," scattered. Then they eat. Bread passed. Milk poured. Eggs halved. The sound of living returns—gently, hesitantly.

PIERRE
(rushing, unsettled) Madame Courbet took my hand —
said she was sorry. Couldn't even look at me.
Stood there wringing her scarf like it was my neck she wanted to
wring—

JEAN
(low) They didn't look at any of us.
Not even the priest.

MARGOT
Someone left milk on the steps.
Blue thread around the jug.

JACQUES
(quiet) Mercy.

They eat. Slowly. With care, but no ease.

MARGOT
Will they say a Mass?

JEAN
(soft) Not for her.

MARGOT
Why not?

ISABELLE
Because they believe she was a heretic.
And they will go on believing —
unless the Holy Father says otherwise.

MARGOT
(after a pause) We could say one.
Here.

> *No one answers. No one argues.*

ISABELLE
Eat, child.
Before it gets cold.

> *Bread passed. Salt pinched. Quiet chewing. They let the moment stay unspoken.*

PIERRE
(bitter rush) We should be in Rouen.
With stones.
With knives in our fists
and God's name rotting on our tongues.

ISABELLE
Go, then.

PIERRE
Don't you want them to pay?

ISABELLE
I want us to eat in peace.

> *A quiet beat. Someone pours more milk. Someone peels another egg.*

JEAN
(soft, remembering) She called on Christ.
And Mother.
And the wind.

PIERRE
They don't care about Christ—only robes and gold,
not the prayers of a girl burning in daylight!

JEAN
She begged for mercy.

PIERRE
(low, savage) And the Bishop said, "Amen."
I should've slit his tongue
and nailed it to the cathedral door
before he could defile her.

ISABELLE
And they'd still call him holy.
(notices MARGOT's stillness) What's wrong with you, girl?

MARGOT
It hurts to swallow.

> *MARGOT looks at her plate but doesn't touch it
> again. The others do not comfort her. But they hear her.*

PIERRE
(gritting it out) Nineteen years old.
And they burned her,
while the Bishop prayed fat prayers
and the guards laughed like drunk men in a brothel.

> *A long pause. No one eats. ISABELLE presses her
> palms flat against the table—as if holding the house
> together. MARGOT weeps quietly. She keeps her hands
> in her lap. PIERRE pushes his plate across the table.*

PIERRE
Why are we even sitting here?

JEAN
(soft, to ISABELLE) You don't have to keep doing this.

ISABELLE
I do.

PIERRE
What's left is ashes.

ISABELLE
What's left is what they couldn't kill.

PIERRE
Then let's name them!

JACQUES
(bitter, broken) You're gutting ghosts.

ISABELLE
(cold, steady) Name her first.

JEAN
(quiet, anchoring) Jeannette.

> *Beat.*

ISABELLE
Say it again.

JEAN
(stronger) Jeannette.

PIERRE
(a cracked prayer) Jeannette.

MARGOT
(a whisper, almost to herself) ...Jeannette.

From the far end of the table, JACQUES exhales a sob. He pushes his plate slightly away and covers his face with one hand. He does not leave the table. No one speaks. The family stays seated. It is the first time they have said her name since they lost her.

ISABELLE
(quietly) Let it simmer.

Lights change.

ACT II

SCENE 1

June 15, 1435

The kitchen. Afternoon pressing into dusk. The fire low.
Pierre works at an oxen's yoke. Jean whittles. The
silence is not hostile—but thick. Shared. The kind that
knows how to breathe between men who have said very
little and lost very much.

PIERRE
This bow's warped.

JEAN
Been warped. You just didn't see it.

PIERRE
She would've.
She saw everything.

JEAN
(smiling fondly) Remember the pigs?

PIERRE
Which time?

JEAN
The day she let them out. Said they looked sad.
Stood back and opened the gate like she was releasing prisoners.

PIERRE
I chased one to the edge of the woods.
She shouted after me, said they wanted to see the trees.

JEAN
And she baptized the littlest one.

Named it Father Luc.
Used the last of the rainwater and Maman's best towel.

A breath. Pierre sets the yoke down gently.

JEAN
Back behind the orchard—she used to corral frogs.
Not to catch them. Just to watch them jump.

PIERRE
Came back with mud up to her knees.
Hair full of burrs.
Said the frogs knew secrets.

JEAN
She kept that snail shell in her pocket,
said she could hear heaven through it.

PIERRE
You told her it was just wind.

JEAN
She told me I had no imagination.

Beat.

PIERRE
She sang to the hens.
Said they laid better if they felt loved.

Long silence. The kind that doesn't need to be filled.
Then—

JEAN
She was barefoot in the frost the morning she left.
Said cold made her feel real.

Pierre doesn't speak. Something in his jaw shifts.

JEAN
I was there.

PIERRE
Don't.

JEAN
She stood there, bound to the stake.
Hair hacked.
She looked so small.
Like the girl who used to sing to the hens.

Beat.

Her eyes were wide open.

PIERRE
(pause.) Did she see you?

JEAN
Yes.
(swallows) She called my name.

Long silence. Pierre turns. Looks at him fully now.

PIERRE
I wasn't there.

JEAN
I know.

PIERRE
I left the night before.

Beat.

JEAN
The flames went up fast.

She begged.
Jesus. Mary.
Anyone.

Pierre is frozen.

JEAN
The bishop watched.

PIERRE
You should've stopped it.

JEAN
And you should've stayed.

They stare at each other. It doesn't become a fight. It becomes a grief too heavy to hold.

PIERRE
We failed her.

JEAN
Yes.

PIERRE
I tell stories about her now.
Armor. Banners. Faith.
But when I sleep—
It's the fire I see.

JEAN
They tried to erase her.
After she died, I thought they would take down her remains.
That we could bring her home and bury her.
But instead, they lit the pyre again.
And then again, once more,
Until there was nothing left.

I wanted to bring home a lock of her hair
Maybe a piece of bone or cloth.

> *Silence.*

PIERRE
Do you think she knew?

JEAN
That we loved her?

PIERRE
That we let them.

> *A long, long silence. Jean turns to the hearth. The pot hisses once. The Earth keeps spinning.*

JEAN
They burned her.
But not all of her.

PIERRE
What's left?

JEAN
This.

> *Long beat.*

We are what happened to her.

> *They don't look at each other. But they don't move apart. The fire does not roar. But it does not go out.*

SCENE 2

Friday, June 12, 1440.

Dusk.

The kitchen has cooled. What warmth remains lives in the stones and the fire's low breath. Shadows stretch long. A stool lies on its side near the hearth. JACQUES, kneeling.

JACQUES
This damn leg again.

ISABELLE
(entering from interior) Because you used pine.

JACQUES
Didn't have oak.

ISABELLE
You had time.

JACQUES
Did I?

Beat.

ISABELLE
You could've asked Pierre to do it.

JACQUES
He'd've made it worse.
Boy swings a hammer like it owes him money.

JACQUES grunts. Shifts to reset the stool. Misses.

JACQUES
These hands used to know the work.
Now I can't even feel the nail.

> *ISABELLE looks over from the hearth—soft.*

ISABELLE
When did you last eat?

JACQUES
I don't know.

> *He lowers himself to sit on the floor. His knees crack.*
> *He presses a hand to his chest—casual, like testing a*
> *bruise.*

ISABELLE
Jacques?

JACQUES
Just tired.
Not cold—not hungry.
Just... tired.

> *ISABELLE crosses to him, slowly.*

ISABELLE
That stool's more stubborn than the rest of us.

JACQUES
That's why she liked it.
(smiles—faintly.) She used to stand on it to stir the pot.
Said it made her feel taller than God.

ISABELLE
She spilled stew on your tax ledgers.
You threatened to excommunicate her.

JACQUES
I should've.
Would've kept her safe.

> *JACQUES exhales. Then grimaces and slumps to the floor.*

ISABELLE
Let me get you some water.

JACQUES
No—stay.
Just sit with me a bit longer.
(beat) She was small, wasn't she, Belle?
Hands like sparrow wings.
Always fluttering.
Couldn't sit still a minute.
Always gathering, mending, chasing the damned hens.
(beat) Remember how she'd stomp out barefoot into the frost?
Mornings so cold you could hear the wood groan—
and there she was, laughing like a fool.
Said it made her feel alive.
We used to think she'd catch her death, but she didn't care.
(smiling) She sang when she worked.
Old songs.
The ones you taught her,
before her hands got busy and her heart got heavy.
(ong breath) And when the church bells rang —
she'd throw down whatever she was carrying and run.
Like she was late for a feast.
(quiet) That was our Jeannette.
Before her angels took her from us.
(beat) Ma mère. Je serai bientôt là, maman. Je suis si heureux de voir ton visage rayonnant.

> *JACQUES cries out, grips his chest. Then, lies still.*

ISABELLE
Margot!

MARGOT appears in the doorway.

ISABELLE
Run. Fetch the priest. Now.

*MARGOT stares—frozen for just a breath—then
bolts. ISABELLE shifts. Cradles Jacques more
fully.*

ISABELLE
Breathe slow.

JACQUES
Didn't expect it to end like this.
Crooked stool.
(beat) Your apron in my face.

ISABELLE
Better than the battlefield.

JACQUES
I never got that far.
Never left the parish, really.

ISABELLE
You came home.
When the day was done.

JACQUES
Too late.

ISABELLE
But you came. *(brushes the hair back from his forehead)*
You were the stone that held the heat.

JACQUES

(a whisper) And you were the one who knew where to stand.

> *He exhales. Once. Then again, long and sustained.*
> *Then not again. ISABELLE holds him. Still. The fire*
> *breathes low. MARGOT returns, breathless, gasping at*
> *the door.*

MARGOT

Madame —

The priest is gone to Orléans.

He won't return until tomorrow.

> *Silence. Heavy. Absolute. ISABELLE closes her eyes*
> *briefly. Then opens them—steady.*

ISABELLE

We have no holy oil, only the lamp.

Fetch it, Margot.

> *MARGOT runs to the back room. ISABELLE runs*
> *her fingers through Jacques' hair. She closes his eyes with*
> *great tenderness. MARGOT returns with the oil lamp.*
> *Sets it carefully beside ISABELLE.*

ISABELLE

We are lowly women.

But God hears the broken.

> *She dips her fingers into the oil. Crosses JACQUES'*
> *forehead—slow, deliberate.*

ISABELLE

(soft, sure) By this holy anointing,

and His most loving mercy,

may the Lord pardon you

whatever wrong you have done

(touches his eyelids) by sight,
(touches his ears) by hearing,
(touches his lips) by word,
(touches his hands) by deed.

> *She crosses herself slowly—forehead, chest, shoulder to shoulder.*

ISABELLE
Go now in peace, Jacques d'Arc.
Husband.
Father.
Stone I stood on.
Stone I still stand on.

> *Beat.*

ISABELLE
Into Your hands, O Lord,
we commend his spirit.

> *She bows her head briefly. Then rises—slow, aching.*

ISABELLE
Go get Pierre.
And Jean.

> *MARGOT hesitates—still stunned—then exits.*
> *ISABELLE moves slowly to the table. Begins clearing it with care. Quiet. One dish at a time. She picks up Jacques's dish last. Holds it a moment longer than the others. Then places it on top—steady, steady. She places a clean sheet on the table. Fetches the water basin and several clean rags.*
> *She waits.*

INTERMISSION.

ACT III

SCENE 1

> *Orléans, France. October 15, 1455. Early evening.*
>
> *The light through the high windows leans warm and narrow, cast in long gold bands across rich color—the floor covered in a gifted Oriental rug. The furnishings are modest but elegant. The fire glows, but does not dominate. It warms; it does not cook. The walls breathe the hush of better linen and nobler visitors. MARGOT sits near the hearth on a cushioned stool, slowly winding thread into a tidy skein. She wears refined servant garb—dark, pressed, deliberate. Her posture is poised, but not tense. Her hands move. Her eyes are still.*
>
> *ISABELLE sits in a fine chair beside a small table with a wooden box on it. She opens the box. Retrieves a cloth bundle—tied with care. Lifts it to her lap. Opens it. One by one, she removes the contents—relics of a life.*

ISABELLE
(low, holding a dried piece of marshmallow root)
This one she bit when she was teething.

> *ISABELLE lifts a doll's head—cracked, faintly scorched.*

ISABELLE
She found poppets fantomatique.
But kept this one.
Ripped the arms off the first week.

> *MARGOT's thread slows. She watches.*

ISABELLE lifts a small wooden comb—a tooth missing.

ISABELLE
Tangled her hair like a wild thing.
Every morning, I'd try to take out the tangles.
She said, "Maman, stop fighting the wind."

She sets the comb down. Touches it. Lets go. She lifts a scapular—worn, frayed.

ISABELLE
She wore this for seven years.
The ribbon broke and she asked me to fix it.
She left before I got around to it.
It wasn't there to protect her.

She clutches the scapular, kisses it, then lays it gently over the comb. She lifts a snail shell.

ISABELLE
I found this snail shell under her pillow when she was fifteen.
I didn't ask.

She holds the final piece: a yellowed scrap of linen, faintly stained red.

ISABELLE
This is from when the voices first came.
She said her head hurt.
I found her in the straw, bleeding from the nose.
She said, "They're beautiful."

Silence.

ISABELLE arranges the items before the Virgin. Her hands still. Her back straight. JEAN enters quietly.

Older, slower, dignified. He stands behind the chair.
Looks at the small altar.

JEAN
I'm starting to forget her voice.

ISABELLE
(quiet, from the floor) Then pray for remembrance.
"Ask, and ye shall receive, that your joy may be full."

> *A knock at the door. MARGOT rises. Crosses. Opens*
> *it. AGNES stands there—flushed from the road, cloak*
> *damp at the hem, walking stick in hand.*

MARGOT
(startled, amazed) Oh, Madame!

AGNES
(light, quick) No time for marveling, girl!

> *MARGOT steps aside. AGNES enters. Her presence*
> *is real, breathing, alive with urgency.*

ISABELLE
(gasping, crossing to embrace her) You walked all this way?!

AGNES
The pilgrimage arrived this evening.
Saint-Aignan is giving us shelter for the night.

> *Beat.*

ISABELLE
What's happened?

AGNES
(excited, direct) The new priest in Domrémy

Père Émile—young, Roman-trained.
Talks fast, listens even faster.
I spoke with him.
Told him I was a friend of the family.
He said a mother may petition!
He said the Bishop must carry the message.
That's how Rome hears it.

ISABELLE becomes still. JEAN looks up.

JEAN
Petition?

AGNES
To clear her name.
Jeannette's name.

ISABELLE
(low, almost a growl) Resurrect her name.

AGNES
Yes!
Père Émile says people all over are whispering.
They call her a martyr and a saint!

JEAN
Maman, of course you must go.
You're the only one who can.

ISABELLE
(slow, uncertain) I've gotten so old and creaky.
How could I travel so far?

AGNES
You have sons.

JEAN
Of course, you do, Maman!
Pierre has a cart—

A pause.

ISABELLE
(quiet, furious) I will go.
I will speak her name until it deafens them.
(turning to MARGOT) Fetch Pierre.

MARGOT
Yes, Madame.

MARGOT exits.

AGNES
It will take weeks. And the weather is turning.

ISABELLE
Then we must leave first thing.

> *From the next room, a door creaks. Heavy footsteps.*
> *PIERRE enters.*

PIERRE
Leave for where?

> *AGNES, who has stayed poised and humming with*
> *purpose, turns to him—her eyes alive.*

AGNES
Paris.

PIERRE
(startled) Now?

> *AGNES nods fast, a smile cracking like kindling.*

AGNES

The new priest, Père Émile, says a mother may petition.
Rome will listen. The Bishop must carry the words.
And your mother, God help them, she's ready to speak.

> *AGNES kisses MARGOT on the forehead, light and sure.*

AGNES

Keep the fire burning steady.

> *She exits swiftly. The door doesn't slam. It exhales. Movement blooms in her wake.*

JEAN

(to PIERRE) We'll take your cart. You'll drive—Marin won't obey anyone else.

PIERRE

He's a scoundrel, that horse.

JEAN

I'll ride in back with Maman. Brace the axle. Pack the straw deep.

PIERRE

Yes, we'll need extra straw and lambskins to cushion the ride for Maman. Margot—steep willow bark, a lot of it, to dull the pain in her joints - and pack the horehound Agnes left. Mint too, for her stomach. And food. Three weeks' worth—dried apples, rye bread, hard cheese, salt meat. No milk. Vinegar and watered wine.

MARGOT

Oui, Monsieur.

ISABELLE

Where will we sleep?

JEAN
I will go speak with Père Émile. I'll ask him for a letter of introduction.
We will stay at churches and convents.

ISABELLE
I will bring proof.
Marriage certificate.
Jeannette's baptism.
Her first communion.
Confirmation.

> *She lifts the baptismal certificate—paper stained at one corner—and holds it like a relic.*

ISABELLE
Her name is still written in the Church's hand.

> *She hands the papers to JEAN. He wraps them in oilcloth with reverence.*

PIERRE
We leave at dawn. Marin's hooves will crack the frost.

> *ISABELLE crosses to the taper. Lights it.*

ISABELLE
(to MARGOT) When I'm gone—

MARGOT
I will keep it lit.

ISABELLE
(quietly, to the taper) My name is Isabelle, widow of Jacques....

> *Lighting shifts.*

SCENE 2

November 10, 1455
Notre Dame Cathedral, Paris

The candles have burned low.
The hearth glows only faintly—embers beneath the
stillness.
The relics remain, untouched.

MARGOT sits in shadow, working in silence.

ISABELLE rises. Moves slowly.

She takes a shawl from the back of the chair—black,
heavy, ceremonial in its plainness.
She puts it over her hair and shoulders.

She steps into a pool of light.
It is not theatrical.
It is clean.
True.
A circle of testimony.

ISABELLE
I am Isabelle.
Widow of Jacques d'Arc.
Mother of Jeannette, the Maid.

I do not come for pity.
I come for justice.

I come because silence has teeth.
And it has gnawed at me long enough.

My daughter was born in lawful marriage.
She was baptized in Domrémy.

I raised her in the fear of God,
and the reverence of the Church.

She spun wool.
She helped her father in the fields.
She confessed often.
She gave alms.

When she was thirteen,
she said she heard voices.

I feared it at first.
But it was not madness.

She changed.
And I was too small to change with her.

Her father said,
"If I knew she would go with soldiers,
I would drown her myself."

But she stood firm.
She said:
"God wills it."

She touches her lips softly. Closes her eyes.

She kissed me before she left.
"Maman, do not fear.
I go with God."

I never saw her again.

Later, we heard she had been taken.

Tried.
Burned.

The Bishop watched.
They condemned her
without mercy,
without aid,
without right.

They made her die most cruelly —
by fire.

But I —
who gave her life —
have come to clear her name.

They said she lied.
No.
She spoke from firm belief.

Beat.

It's not faith that burns a girl.

It's fear.
It's cowardice.
It's the hands that sign verdicts and call them holy.

She was innocent.
She was devout.
SHE was holy.

And if there is any justice left —
you will write her name clean.

Remember not the fire, but the girl.
Not the ashes —
but the breath she used to say:
"God is with me."

ISABELLE does not move. Her body stays upright, rooted.

Lights change.

EPILOGUE

MARGOT
(quiet, clear) Because a mother spoke —
the walls of the Church cracked open.

Her cry for justice would not be ignored.

Within days, Pope Calixtus III ordered an inquiry.

Over the next year, more than a hundred witnesses rose:
Knights.
Priests.
Peasants.
Soldiers.
Guards.

They revealed the lies.
The chains.
The rape.
The fire.

They unmade the Bishop's verdict—thread by thread.
They named her innocent.
They named her holy.
The woman who bore her
asked not for sainthood
Only Truth.

The name they tried to burn away
rose higher than any throne:

Joan of Arc.

END OF PLAY

PLAYWRIGHT'S NOTE

Joan of Arc is my patron saint.

I am a Cradle Catholic. Catholicism was not just the religion we practiced, it was the air my foremothers breathed. It shaped how we marked time, how we held grief, how we defined womanhood. It lived in kitchen prayers, sacramental silences, and the muscle-memory of faith passed from mother to daughter not through sermons, but through bread, beads, and burden.

Joan of Arc lived in that world—a girl in armor, a saint in glass. The virgin martyr. She was always there. But I didn't know her.

Not until I saw Carl Theodor Dreyer's *The Passion of Joan of Arc*. Her eyes, wide and burning, opened something in me that would not close. I began to read the transcripts—from both her first (sham) trial and the nullification trial that followed. Joan was illiterate. But she *spoke*, and her voice was recorded by men who tried to twist and condemn her. She could not write, but her words burned through parchment just the same.

I hadn't known her mother fought to clear her name—and won.
That 115 witnesses rose to defend her.
That she was exonerated in 1456.
That the Church later called her first trial "tainted by deception, malice, and manifest injustice."
That her body was burned three times, her ashes cast into the Seine to prevent veneration.

This play is born from those revelations.

Even Unto Death does not dramatize Joan's voices or victories. It stays with those left behind: her grieving, unrelenting mother Isabelle; the servant girl Margot, who saw too much; the men in the house, broken by their silence. The play asks not only what happened to Joan, but why it was allowed—and who dared to remember.

Joan was not fearless. That myth is convenient. She was nineteen. Imprisoned. Alone. Terrified. They threatened her with torture, with death, with lifelong imprisonment and—though rarely acknowledged—rape at the hands of guards and jailers. Her "choice" was not noble. It was impossible. And she chose fire. Not because she did not fear it, but because she could not endure a life in secular prison.

In 1920, Joan of Arc was canonized. But not for her courage, nor for her visions. For her virginity.

Even her most radical act—wearing men's clothes—was both spiritual and fiercely personal. Joan vowed never to share her body with a man. She bound herself to God and held to that vow with unflinching clarity. Her clothes weren't merely protection. They were resistance. Her way of saying: *this body is mine; I serve God alone.*

But the Church sanctified her only through the narrowest frame —chastity. They erased her fire, her voice, her defiance. They made her safe. They made her still. They made her saintly.

As feminist theologian Rosemary Radford Ruether wrote, "They could only make Joan a saint by stripping her of everything that made her dangerous."

This pattern is familiar. The Blessed Mother is venerated for her obedience and perpetual virginity. Joan becomes holy not because she rebelled, but because she remained "untouched." And girls like Margot, who survive what others won't name, are left outside the realm of sanctity altogether.

This play rejects that division. It remembers Isabelle Romée, the mother who spoke up. The one who refused to let her daughter be erased.

I wrote this play to illuminate the truth about a girl who has been with me all my life. Not because she was fearless, but because she *wasn't.* And because her mother fought for her, as so many mothers including mine, heaven rest her, didn't. — *Jeanmarie Simpson*

ABOUT THE PLAYWRIGHT

Jeanmarie Simpson is an American theatre artist whose plays center women who challenge power structures—political, religious, and psychological. Her solo and ensemble works explore grief, justice, memory, and resistance. Her theatrical language blurs the sacred and the personal.

She is best known for *A Single Woman*, a two-hander about Jeannette Rankin that premiered Off-Broadway at The Culture Project. It was adapted into a film featuring Judd Nelson and the voices of Martin Sheen and Patricia Arquette, with music by Joni Mitchell. Following the film's release, the stage production toured to 53 countries across five continents. The play earned "Best Theatrical Surprise" from *Sacramento News & Review* and was presented at CalArts, where Simpson was a Surdna Distinguished Guest Artist.

Her original works include *HERETIC — The Mary Dyer Story*, *Bambino Mio — Bright Little Flame* (about Maria Montessori), and *The Jewish Question*, which received Honorable Mention from the Jewish Plays Project.

Her work has been supported by six Sierra Arts Foundation grants, twelve from the Nevada Arts Council, and multiple National Endowment for the Arts Theatre awards. In 2022, she received a Living History Foundation grant for *Bambino Mio — Bright Little Flame*. She served as a panelist for the NEA's 2023 Grants for Arts Projects.

She is the Founding Artistic Director of Arizona Theatre Matters and a member of the Dramatists Guild of America. She is retired from the Stage Directors and Choreographers Society, Actors' Equity Association, and SAG-AFTRA.

Published by Upstage Left Press

1209 Mountain Road Pl NE, Suite N

Albuquerque, NM 87110 USA

This collection contains original dramatic works by Jeanmarie Simpson. Any resemblance to real persons, living or dead, is intentional only where noted, and always in the service of theatrical inquiry.

First Edition · 2025

Printed in the United States of America